The Govern[...]

Being an Independent Regulator

OECD

BETTER POLICIES FOR BETTER LIVES

This work is published under the responsibility of the Secretary-General of the OECD. The opinions expressed and arguments employed herein do not necessarily reflect the official views of OECD member countries.

This document and any map included herein are without prejudice to the status of or sovereignty over any territory, to the delimitation of international frontiers and boundaries and to the name of any territory, city or area.

Please cite this publication as:
OECD (2016), *Being an Independent Regulator*, The Governance of Regulators, OECD Publishing, Paris.
http://dx.doi.org/10.1787/9789264255401-en

ISBN 978-92-64-25539-5 (print)
ISBN 978-92-64-25540-1 (PDF)

Series: The Governance of Regulators
ISSN 2415-1432 (print)
ISSN 2415-1440 (online)

The statistical data for Israel are supplied by and under the responsibility of the relevant Israeli authorities. The use of such data by the OECD is without prejudice to the status of the Golan Heights, East Jerusalem and Israeli settlements in the West Bank under the terms of international law.

Photo credits: Cover © Leigh Prather – Fotolia.com.

Corrigenda to OECD publications may be found on line at: *www.oecd.org/about/publishing/corrigenda.htm*.
© OECD 2016

You can copy, download or print OECD content for your own use, and you can include excerpts from OECD publications, databases and multimedia products in your own documents, presentations, blogs, websites and teaching materials, provided that suitable acknowledgement of OECD as source and copyright owner is given. All requests for public or commercial use and translation rights should be submitted to *rights@oecd.org*. Requests for permission to photocopy portions of this material for public or commercial use shall be addressed directly to the Copyright Clearance Center (CCC) at *info@copyright.com* or the Centre français d'exploitation du droit de copie (CFC) at *contact@cfcopies.com*.

Foreword

Regulators can best be described as the "referees" of markets. These public bodies help ensure access to and the quality of key public services, facilitate infrastructure management, including investment, and enhance market efficiency. They play a crucial role in supporting sustainable and inclusive growth while maintaining confidence in markets, which is critical for trust in public institutions. This is no easy task. Regulators operate in a complex environment at the interface among public authorities, the private sector and end-users. As "referees", they must often balance competing wants and needs from different actors through the application of good governance. This means that they must behave and act objectively, impartially, and consistently, without conflict of interest, bias or undue influence.

What makes an independent regulator is not simply institutional design. Moreover, independence does not imply that regulators are anonymous, silent, or above and beyond the policy arena. Regulators interact with ministries, who are ultimately responsible for developing the policies for the regulated sector; with parliaments, who approve those policies and often evaluate their implementation; with the regulated industry, which needs to comply with the decisions of the regulator; and with citizens, who are the ultimate beneficiaries of the actions of governments and regulators. These interactions are inevitable and desirable. The balance between the appropriate and undue influence that can be exercised through these interactions is at the core of the discussion on the independence of regulators.

This report identifies the critical points where undue influence can be exercised by looking at the rationale – *the why* – and the practical implications – *the how* – of independence. It builds on a review of the academic literature to pinpoint why independence matters and what independence is expected to bring. It relies on responses to a survey conducted among 48 regulators of 26 OECD and partner countries across all economic sectors to identify how independence is translated into practice.

The report finds that undue pressure can be exercised at different points in the life of a regulatory agency. Accordingly, independence is not a given. Rather, it needs to be translated into practice throughout the work and life of a regulatory agency. Formal arrangements to safeguard independence can support the emergence of a "culture of independence" within the regulator. However, to be effective, these formal arrangements need to inform the daily work and practice of the regulators' leadership and professional staff. Beyond the regulators' institutional set-up, the way in which regulators attract, retain and motivate staff is a key determinant of the regulators' capacity to act independently and take objective and evidence-based decisions.

Board and agency heads can be under considerable pressure from government and industry as they are ultimately responsible for the regulator's decisions. Accordingly, safeguards and protection from undue pressure on them and the decisions taken by the regulator are paramount. These safeguards should be in place as of the nomination and appointment processes of board and agency heads. They need to extend to the processes and tools used to take decisions, including how formal and informal consultations with government and industry are conducted and used.

Budget allocation and management are also critical points where undue pressure and influence can be exercised. In this respect, particular attention should be paid to the way in which funding needs are determined, appropriated and spent, regardless of the source of funding for regulators.

This report contributes to the OECD work programme on the governance of regulators and regulatory policy led by the OECD Network of Economic Regulators and the OECD Regulatory Policy Committee with the support of the Regulatory Policy Division of the OECD Public Governance and Territorial Development Directorate. The Directorate's mission is to help government at all levels design and implement strategic, evidence-based and innovative policies to strengthen public governance, respond effectively to diverse and disruptive economic, social and environmental challenges and deliver on government's commitments to citizens. The goal is to support countries in building better government systems and implementing policies at both national and regional level that lead to sustainable economic and social development.

Acknowledgements

The work underlying this report was led by Faisal Naru and prepared by Filippo Cavassini and Vivian Leung with the encouragement and support of Rolf Alter, Director, Public Governance and Territorial Development Directorate, and Nick Malyshev, Head, Regulatory Policy Division, Public Governance and Territorial Development Directorate. Luiz De Mello, Deputy Director, Public Governance and Territorial Development Directorate, Nick Malyshev and Cristiana Vitale provided inputs and comments. Jennifer Stein co-ordinated the editorial process.

The members of the OECD Network of Economic Regulators provided comments throughout the preparation of this report and were instrumental in providing the data and information underlying the analysis presented in the report. Thanks are extended to all of them and in particular to Ana Albuquerque, Board Member, Water & Waste Services Regulatory Authority, Portugal, Irene Åmot, Director of the Service Markets Department, Norwegian Communications Authority, Norway, Claudia Barriga Choy, Senior Advisor, Supervisory Agency of Investment in Telecommunications, Peru, Raminta Brazinskaite, Economist, Office of Rail and Road, United Kingdom, Jean Cattan, Advisor, Regulatory Authority for Electronic Communications and Postal Services, France, Ben Coleman, Technical Specialist, National Energy Board, Canada, Cristina Cifuentes, Commissioner, Australian Competition and Consumer Commission, Australia, Antonello De Tommaso, Head of the EU and International Affairs Office, Communications Regulatory Authority, Italy, Nicolò Di Gaetano, Senior Advisor, Regulatory Authority for Electricity, Gas and Water, Italy, Citlalli Ivonne García González, Chief of Multilateral Affairs, Federal Telecommunications Institute, Mexico, Juan Enrique Gradolph Cadierno, International Affairs Director, National Authority for Markets and Competition, Spain, Annegret Groebel, Head of the International Relations and Postal Regulation Department, Federal Network Agency for Electricity, Gas, Telecommunications, Post and Railway, Germany, Eric Kimmel, Director of Regulatory Development & Management, Alberta Energy Regulator, Canada, Aude Le Tellier, Policy Officer, Energy Regulatory Commission, France, Doriana Lucaferri, Institutional and International Affairs, Transport Regulatory Authority, Italy, Jens Lundgren, Deputy Chief Economist, Swedish Energy Markets Inspectorate, Sweden, Jana Mackintosh, Manager, Policy, Payment Systems Regulator, United

Kingdom, Lija Makare, Head of External Relations, Public Utilities Commission, Latvia, Mathieu Meier, Expert, Federal Electricity Commission, Switzerland, Marianne Minnecré-Kracht, Coordinating Strategic Advisor, The Netherlands Authority for Consumers and Markets, The Netherlands, Jean-Yves Ollier, Director General, Energy Regulatory Commission, France, Assunta Luisa Perrotti, Head of Cabinet, Transport Regulatory Authority, Italy, Nicci Russell, Director of Strategy and Planning, Water Services Regulation Authority for England and Wales, United Kingdom, Antoine Samba, Head of the European and International Affairs Directorate, Regulatory Authority for Electronic Communications and Postal Services, France, Francesco Schiacchitano, EU and International Affairs Office, Communications Regulatory Authority, Italy, Jesus Serrano Landeros, Commissioner, Energy Regulatory Commission, Mexico, Mustafa Sezgin, Head of the Strategy and Sectoral Policies Group, Energy Market Regulatory Authority, Turkey, Alan Sutherland, Chief Executive Officer, Water Industry Commission for Scotland, United Kingdom, Katharina Tappeiner, International Policy and Projects, E-Control, Austria, Josée Touchette, Chief Operating Officer, National Energy Board, Canada, Arturo L. Vásquez Cordano, Chief Economist, Supervisory Agency of Investment in Energy and Mining, Peru, Adam Wilson, Chief Executive Officer, Essential Services Commission of South Australia, Australia.

This work was undertaken with the support of the UK Office of Gas and Electricity Markets. Special thanks are extended to Andrew Burgess, Associate Partner, Energy Systems, for encouraging and supporting this work throughout its different stages.

The literature review informing the analysis of the why of independence was conducted in co-operation with the Chair of Governance and Regulation of the Paris-Dauphine University. Special thanks are extended to Professor Eric Brousseau for facilitating this co-operation and to Nevena Zhelyazkova, Post-Doctoral Researcher, who conducted the underlying research on the rationale, determinants and some of the expected outcomes of independence presented in Chapter 2.

An initial draft of the independence survey underlying this work was presented to the OECD Network of Economic Regulators for comments in April 2015. An early draft of the report was discussed at the OECD Network of Economic Regulators in November 2015. The report was presented to the OECD Network of Economic Regulators and the OECD Regulatory Policy Committee for final comments in April 2016.

Table of contents

Acronyms and abbreviations 9
Executive summary 11
Chapter 1. **The why and the how of being an independent regulator** 15
    Purpose 16
    Methodology 19
    Data coverage 20
    The why of independence 21
    The how of independence 24
    References 31
Chapter 2. **Why does independence matter? The view from the literature** 33
    Rationale for independence 34
    Determinants of independence 37
    Outcomes of independence 44
    References 47
Chapter 3. **How does independence work in practice? Key trends and evidence** . 51
    Instructions from the executive 52
    Relationship with industry 61
    Staff 67
    Budget 79
    References 84
Annex A. **Key bibliographical references** 85

Tables

2.1. Theoretical (market failure) arguments for regulatory independence 35
2.2. Features of independence common to academic literature 38
3.1. The reported actors at each stage of the regulatory cycle 52

Figures

1.1. Structure of the independence survey 19
1.2. Independence survey respondents by country 20
1.3. Profile of participating regulatory agencies 21
3.1. Typology of interactions between executives and regulators 53
3.2. Does the government issue formal statements on its expectations of the conduct of the regulator's activities? 54
3.3. How does the government indicate its preferred position regarding regulatory decisions, if it does so? 57
3.4. Typology of interactions between industry and regulators 61
3.5. Direct and indirect stakeholder pressures 64
3.6. Protecting staff from undue influence 67
3.7. Who appoints the regulator's staff? 68
3.8. To whom is senior management responsible to? 69
3.9. Use of ethics codes among regulators 70
3.10. Regulators' remuneration policies 71
3.11. Is it an issue finding competent and skilled staff for an independent organisation? 72
3.12. Restrictions on pre- or post-employment of professional staff 73
3.13. Authority nominating the board/head 75
3.14. Authority appointing the board/head 76
3.15. Is there security of tenure for board members/head? 77
3.16. Are there restrictions on post-employment of board members/head? 78
3.17. Length of cooling-off period for board members/head 78
3.18. Independence entry point for budgeting 79
3.19. Regulators' funding sources 80
3.20. Who sets the regulatory fee? 81
3.21. Timeline of budget appropriations 83

Acronyms and abbreviations

ACCC	Australian Competition and Consumer Commission, Australia
AEEGSI	*Autorità per l'energia elettrica, il gas ed il Sistema idrico*, Regulatory Authority for Electricity, Gas and Water, Italy
AGCOM	*Autorità per le Garanzie nelle Comunicazioni,* Communications Regulatory Authority, Italy
ARCEP	*Autorité de régulation des communications électroniques et des postes*, Regulatory Authority for Electronic Communications and Postal Services, France
ART	*Autorità di Regolazione dei Trasporti,* Transport Regulatory Authority, Italy
BNetzA	*Bundesnetzagentur,* Network Agency for Electricity, Gas, Telecommunications, Post and Railway, Germany
CNH	*Comisión Nacional de Hidrocarburos,* National Hydrocarbons Commission, Mexico
CNMC	*Comisión Nacional de los Mercados y la Competencia* National Authority for Markets and Competition, Spain
COAG EC	Council of Australian Governments Energy Council, Australia
CRE France	*Commission de régulation de l'énergie*, Energy Regulatory Commission, France
CRE Mexico	*Comisión Reguladora de Energía*, Energy Regulatory Commission, Mexico
Defra	Department of Environment, Food, and Rural Affairs, United Kingdom
ElCom	Federal Electricity Commission, Switzerland
EMRA	Energy Market Regulatory Authority, Turkey
EPRA	European Platform of Regulatory Agencies
ERGA	European Regulators Group for Audio-Visual Media Services
ERRA	Energy Regulators Regional Association

ERSAR	*Entidade Reguladora does Servicios de Aguas e Residuos,* Water and Waste Services Regulation Authority, Portugal
ESCOSA	Essential Services Commission of South Australia, Australia
GRACO	*Groupe d'échange entre l'ARCEP, les collectivités territoriales et les opérateurs,* Consultative group between the ARCEP, local governments and operators, France
IFT	*Instituto Federal de Telecomunicaciones,* Federal Institute of Telecommunications, Mexico
NEB	National Energy Board of Canada
NER	Network of Economic Regulators
Nkom	Norwegian Communications Authority
Ofgem	Office of Gas and Electricity Markets, United Kingdom
Ofwat	Water Services Regulation Authority for England and Wales
Osinergmin	*Organismo Supervisor de la Inversión en Energía y Minería,* Supervisory Agency of Investment in Energy and Mining, Peru
Osiptel	*Organismo Supervisor de Inversión Privada en Comunicaciones,* Supervisory Agency of Investment in Telecommunications, Peru
PAFER	Performance Assessment Framework for Economic Regulators
PMR	Product Market Regulation
PSR	Payment Systems Regulator, United Kingdom
PUC	Public Utilities Commission, Latvia
R&D	Research and development
RM	Regulatory Management
SoE	Statement of Expectations
SoI	Statement of Intent

Executive summary

Good governance practice requires assigning the right functions to appropriate and capable public institutions. There is value in separating some regulatory functions in public bodies, especially those related to administering or implementing regulation, from the policy-setting and fiscal policy functions that are exercised by government. The independence of these public bodies can contribute to the better functioning of the sectors and markets they oversee.

However, fully understanding the determinants of independence across different market contexts is difficult. There have been few attempts to analyse some of the practical implications and features of independence, beyond institutional set-up, and how these features are practiced by regulators. The independence survey conducted among members of the OECD Network of Economic Regulators fills this gap.

Forty-eight regulators of 26 OECD and partner countries across all economic sectors responded to the survey, providing unique information on the organisational, relational and contextual aspects informing the actual behaviour of regulatory agencies.

Survey responses show that the balance between due and undue influence is at the heart of the debate on the independence of regulators. Critical points for preventing undue influence include:

Instructions from the executive

- In some instances the lack of clarity on roles and functions can open the door to undue government interventions. Some degree of overlapping is inevitable and intrinsic. However, confusion and ensuing deadlocks should be avoided, for example, by identifying in advance possible problematic areas and having regular exchanges on possible solutions between the executive and regulators.
- Grey areas will inevitably remain between the executive and the regulator. The legislative process and parliament can be useful in clarifying these grey areas and resolving possible deadlocks.

Regular dialogue between regulators and parliament can inform parliamentarians on the role of regulators and facilitate an informed debate when issues emerge.

- The use of public consultations can help regulators obtain and disclose the views of the executive in an open and accountable way. Informal and regular exchange of information could also be an effective way of complementing more formal channels of communication. However, these exchanges should be made transparent when appropriate.

- Media statements go beyond the usual institutional channels of communication between government and regulators and can become a solution of "last resort" either to exercise some influence on regulators or to respond to attempts by government to unduly influence the work of the regulator. The media can serve as a useful, transparent reminder of the respective roles of the regulator and the executive. However, in the absence of a pluralistic media landscape, their useful role can be seriously diminished.

- Some regulators have been proactive in scanning the markets they oversee and signalling emerging issues. This proactivity could be perceived as an encroachment on the prerogatives of the executive, unless handled well. Sometimes it might be more appropriate for regulators to signal upcoming issues in advance to ministries. Where ministries lack the political or administrative capacity, regulators should be enabled with a legitimate mechanism for strategic foresight.

Relationship with industry and other non-government stakeholders

- Transparency and consultation can help ensure that decisions build on a wide range of evidence and are perceived as reflecting the needs and the legitimate demands of industry and users. However, consultation can also be hijacked by powerful lobby groups. In these cases, transparency could undermine or curtail the regulators' independence.

- Consultation can become erroneously conflated in the public's mind with consensus. This can create unrealistic expectations among stakeholders. Informed participation by stakeholders could help dispel some of this confusion. Clear timelines for consultation could also help avoid prolonged or untimely interference in the decision-making process (as well as deadlock).

- Some consultations can be very technical and only of interest to a few interested parties. Innovative processes should be developed that enable regulators to conduct due diligence without wasting resources, in line with existing legal obligations. There should be a balance between having accountability for regulatory decisions and "gaming" of the regulatory process.

- Stakeholders can also try to influence regulators' decisions through lobbying. Lobbying rules can help regulators make the relationship with industry more transparent. More problematic are the cases where stakeholders can exercise pressures on ministers and members of parliament to affect the regulator's decisions. Some regulators have counteracted these pressures by going public on these issues.

Staff

- The way in which the regulators attract, retain and motivate staff is ultimately a key determinant of the ability of the regulator to act independently and take decisions that are objective and evidence-based. The culture of professionalism accompanied by "soft" incentives have somewhat compensated for the remuneration gap with the industry.

- A number of regulators have conflict-of-interest policies and cooling-off periods for staff leaving the organisation. These policies signal a clear and useful distinction between the regulator and the regulated industry. However, cooling-off periods can also create perverse incentives. Some of these incentives can be minimised by having some compensation during the cooling-off period.

- Board and agency heads are inevitably under more pressure from government and industry as they are ultimately responsible for the regulator's decisions. The nomination process (rather than the appointment) is a crucial juncture where independent panels for selecting nominees can help foster a culture of independence.

Budget

- The source of funding – fees, general revenues or a mix of the two – is less important than the way in which funding needs are determined, appropriated and spent. Most regulators' budgets are part of the national budget, which is a guarantee of transparency and accountability of regulators to citizens, and can strengthen independence.

- For regulators funded through fees, an appropriate cost-recovery mechanism is essential to set the "right" fee and avoid a regulator that is under-funded, captured by industry or undermined by the executive (for example in countries with large regulated state-owned enterprises).

- For regulators funded through general revenues, it can be easier to influence the regulator by reducing the resources at the disposal of the regulator. Annual appropriations can make it easier to influence the regulator than multi-annual appropriations that are less contingent to short-term political/electoral imperatives. Adequate safeguards should be in place so that the budget process does not become a tool to unduly direct the regulator.

Chapter 1

The why and the how of being an independent regulator

Understanding the benefits, challenges and the practical implications of independence is crucial for the performance of the regulator. However, fully understanding these different aspects of independence can be difficult. This chapter presents the methodology adopted to address some of these difficulties. It provides an overview of what independence is expected to bring to regulators and some key insights on the practical requirements and practices in place to safeguard independence.

Purpose

Independence does not mean that regulators are "anonymous… silent… above… over… beyond the System".* Regulators are key players in the policy arena with an active role in implementing public policies (Box 1.1). It is inevitable and desirable that regulators interact with ministries, who are ultimately responsible for developing the policies for the regulated sector; parliaments, who approve those policies and often evaluate their implementation; the regulated industry, which need to comply with the decisions of the regulator; and citizens, who are the ultimate beneficiaries of the actions of governments and regulators. Understanding the benefits, challenges and the practical implications of independence is therefore crucial for the performance of the regulator.

Box 1.1. What is a regulator?

The *OECD Best Practice Principles on the Governance of Regulators* define a regulator as an entity authorised by statute to use legal tools to achieve policy objectives, imposing obligations or burdens through functions such as licensing, permitting, accrediting, approvals, inspection and enforcement. A regulator can use other complementary tools such as information campaigns, to achieve the policy objectives, but it is the exercise of control through legal powers that makes the integrity of their decision-making processes, and thus their governance, very important.

There are a number of different types of regulators with different roles and responsibilities – among others, economic, financial, overseeing competition and/or consumer protection or setting technical standards and/or a mix of some of these roles. This report focuses on economic regulators and regulators with both economic and competition/consumer protection responsibilities. While the sector and the responsibilities of a regulator can affect the relevance of some of the issues discussed in this report, these issues, including what is appropriate influence of the political power, regulated industry and other stakeholders can apply to all regulators.

Source: OECD (2014), *The Governance of Regulators*, OECD Best Practice Principles for Regulatory Policy, OECD Publishing, Paris, http://dx.doi.org/10.1787/9789264209015-en.

---

*. Regulators are not Men in Black, who will "not stand out in any way. Your entire image is crafted to leave no lasting memory with anyone you encounter. […] Anonymity is your name. Silence your native tongue. You're no longer part of the System. You're above the System. Over it. Beyond it." From the film "The Men in Black" (United States, 1997), directed by Barry Sonnenfeld.

This report responds to the request from members of the Network of Economic Regulators to better understand the practical implications of independence for regulators (Box 1.2).

> **Box 1.2. The OECD Network of Economic Regulators**
>
> What makes a "world-class regulator"? The OECD Network of Economic Regulators (NER) has been addressing this question through objective data, rigorous analysis and dialogue. A subsidiary body of the OECD Regulatory Policy Committee, the NER facilitates peer-to-peer learning and exchange of experience across approximately 80 regulators from OECD members and non-members responsible for network sectors such as communications, electricity, gas, payment services, transport and water.
>
> The work of the NER builds on the recognition that governance matters to ensure good regulatory outcomes and the delivery of essential services to citizens. The NER has contributed to developing the *2014 OECD Best Practice Principles on the Governance of Regulators* (OECD, 2014) to help regulators assess their governance arrangements and strengthen their performance. It has contributed to improving the relevance and focus of the first Product Market Regulator Survey on Regulatory Management of Network Regulators, which look at formal arrangements for independence, accountability and scope of action of regulators overseeing energy, telecommunications, rail, air transport and ports. In parallel, specific work on water has identified the governance arrangements of water regulators, based on a survey of 34 regulators. The NER has also developed a Performance Assessment Framework for Economic Regulators (PAFER) for reviewing regulators' efforts towards measuring their own performance, which is being applied to a number of NER members, including regulators in Colombia, Latvia and Mexico.
>
> *Source*: OECD (2014), *The Governance of Regulators*, OECD Best Practice Principles for Regulatory Policy, OECD Publishing, Paris, http://dx.doi.org/10.1787/9789264209015-en; OECD (2016a), "The OECD Network of Economic Regulators", www.oecd.org/gov/regulatory-policy/ner.htm (accessed 15 April 2016).

At a roundtable on the independence of regulators organised during the 4th meeting of the NER in April 2015, NER members discussed the rationale, practical implications and impact of independence on regulated sectors. The discussion highlighted:

- **Long-term regulatory stability**: regulators can help align the interests of users and, more broadly, citizens and society with the interests of investors in key sectors like energy, water, transport and telecommunications. Independence from the executive government (which would, for example, require specific procedures for agency head/board appointments and dismissals, protection from political influence on regulatory decisions and some autonomy in managing human and financial resources) can shield regulators from short-term party politics and help ensure a stable and credible regulatory environment that facilitates long-term investment. If protecting regulators from the "undue" influence of the executive can strengthen investors' confidence, it is equally important that regulators do not fall prey to "undue" influence from the regulated industry or be captured by the narrow interests that could be expressed by consumer groups, especially when consulting on regulatory decisions. The integrity of the regulator vis-à-vis industry helps address the shortcomings that usually characterise these markets (e.g. monopolistic power and asymmetric information) and make the best use of available resources. It is equally important for ensuring trust of citizens (i.e. the end users of network industries) in an unbiased regulatory environment where regulators are also not captured by powerful consumer lobbying groups (either directly or indirectly through other pressure from other parts of government): users can thus make decisions that fit their preferences and provide the "right" signals to markets.

- **Role clarity and accountability**: independence does not mean that regulators will work in a vacuum, without appropriate checks on their work or disconnected from executive government's decisions. Independence is hard to realise if the roles and respective responsibilities of the executive government and regulators are unclear and ill-defined. Little clarity on the respective roles creates "grey areas" where the decisions on policy priorities and objectives (the responsibility of elected governments) are mixed with regulatory decisions that should contribute to achieving these objectives (the responsibility of independent regulators). Setting clear and transparent boundaries on who does what and which institution can be held accountable is essential to guarantee independence of regulatory agencies and make them accountable for what they do.

- **Changes**: independence is not a static given. The composition and preferences of executive governments (and parliaments) change and, ultimately, these institutions retain the responsibility for the institutional framework of regulatory agencies. Regulated sectors tend to evolve rapidly, responding to technological change and changing user preferences. In such a dynamic institutional and economic environment, a deeper understanding of the practical implications of independence and how to realise it is paramount, not only for regulators but also for executive governments and other stakeholders.

Methodology

The report draws on a *literature review* prepared in co-operation with the Chair of Governance and Regulation of the Paris-Dauphine University to present the rationale, determinants and some of the expected outcomes of independence (Chapter 2). To identify some of the practical implications of independence (Chapter 3), the report draws on the answers provided by NER members to an independence survey that includes a set of *practical questions on the independence of regulators* and was circulated among NER members between July and October 2015.

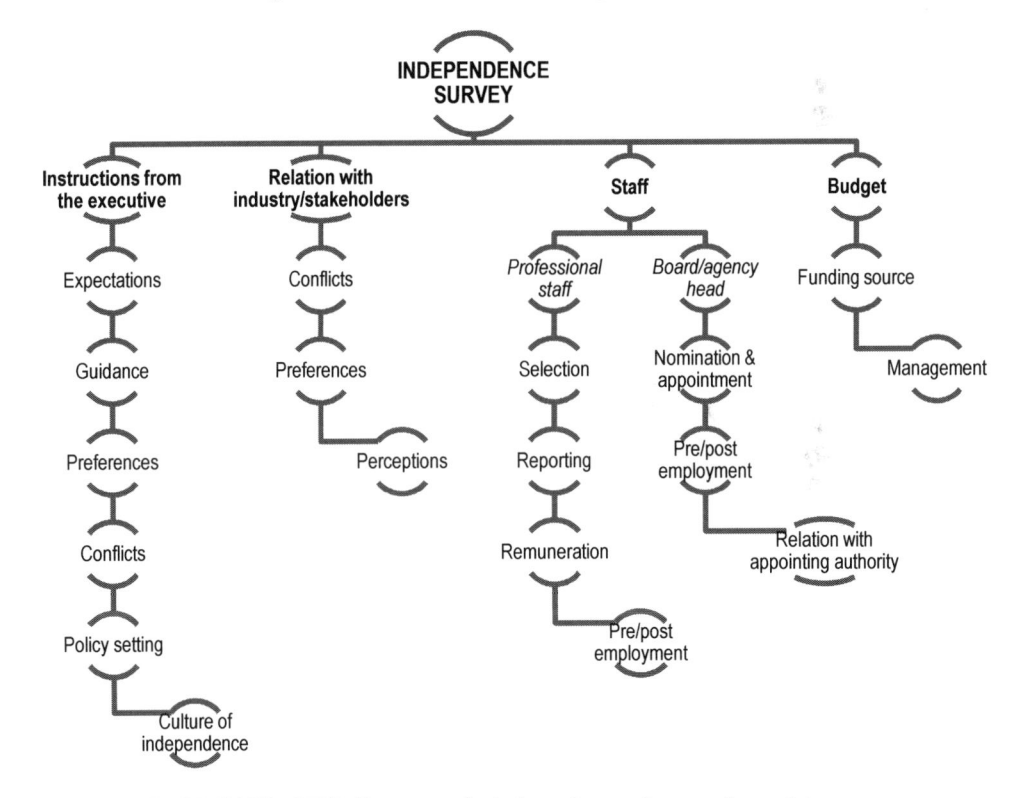

Figure 1.1. **Structure of the independence survey**

```
                              INDEPENDENCE
                                SURVEY
    ┌─────────────────┬─────────────────────┬──────────────────┬──────────────┐
 Instructions from   Relation with           Staff              Budget
 the executive       industry/stakeholders
    │                     │              ┌──────┬──────┐         │
 Expectations         Conflicts      Professional  Board/agency  Funding source
    │                     │           staff         head          │
 Guidance             Preferences        │            │         Management
    │                     │           Selection    Nomination &
 Preferences          Perceptions        │         appointment
    │                                Reporting        │
 Conflicts                               │         Pre/post
    │                                Remuneration  employment
 Policy setting                          │            │
    │                                 Pre/post    Relation with
 Culture of                          employment   appointing authority
 independence
```

Source: OECD (2015), OECD Survey on the independence of economic regulators.

The survey contains mostly descriptive data on *de facto* and some *de jure* arrangements supporting the independence of regulators. To deepen the body of knowledge already collected through the Product Market Regulation – Regulatory Management (PMR – RM) dataset, the survey is structured around the same themes that were surveyed for the independence section of the PMR – RM dataset plus a section on the relationship with stakeholders, which was included at the request of NER members. An early draft of the survey was discussed at the 4th meeting of the NER. The final survey reflects extensive inputs from NER members (Figure 1.1).

Data coverage

Forty-eight regulators from 26 countries completed the independence survey questionnaire. Respondents included 18 OECD countries, 3 accession countries (Colombia, Latvia and Lithuania) and 5 non-members (Albania, Oman, Peru, Russia and South Africa). For eight countries, more than one regulator responded to the questionnaire. Respondents included also five sub-national regulators from Australia and Canada (Figure 1.2).

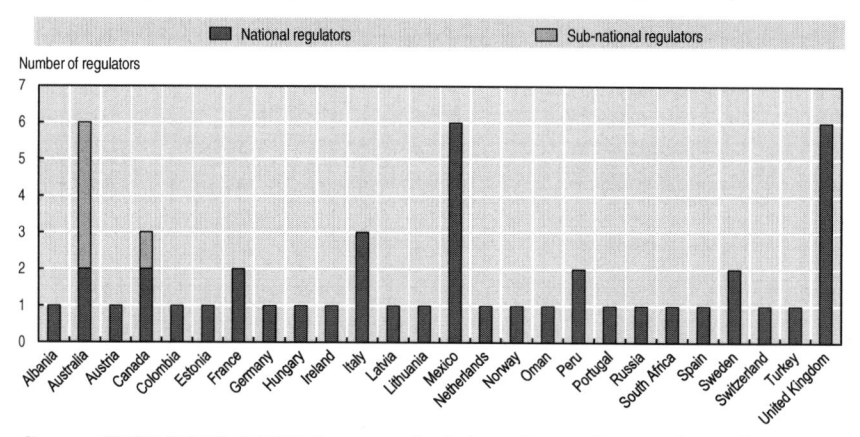

Figure 1.2. **Independence survey respondents by country**

Source: OECD (2015), OECD Survey on the independence of economic regulators.

A diverse mix of regulators is represented in the results, ranging from single-sector regulators to regulators that have both sector and competition functions. Participating regulators are mostly responsible for a single sector (70%), the majority of which oversee energy regulations, followed by communications, transport, water, and payment services. Two dual-sector regulators are responsible for both water and waste management sectors. There are also seven multi-sector regulators included, as well as five regulators with both sector and competition functions (Figure 1.3).

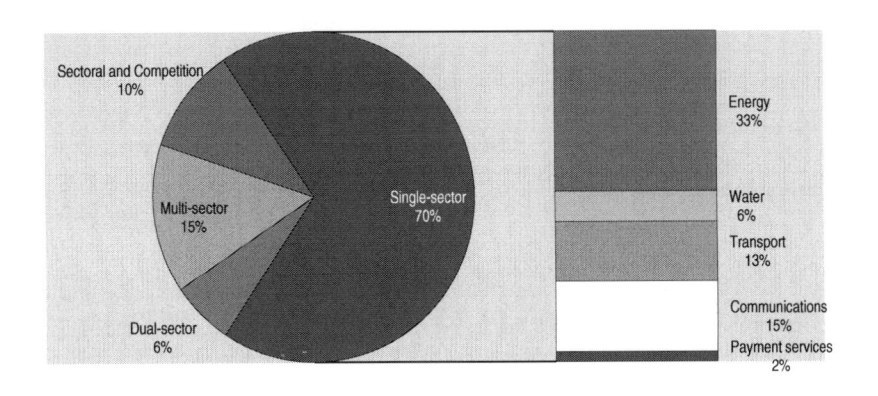

Figure 1.3. **Profile of participating regulatory agencies**

- Sectoral and Competition: 10%
- Multi-sector: 15%
- Single-sector: 70%
- Dual-sector: 6%
- Energy: 33%
- Water: 6%
- Transport: 13%
- Communications: 15%
- Payment services: 2%

Source: OECD (2015), OECD Survey on the independence of economic regulators.

The why of independence

Rationale

There is value in separating some of the regulatory functions, especially those related to administering regulation, from the policy-setting and fiscal policy functions that are exercised by government. Regulation is expected to mitigate market failures at minimum cost. Independence of regulatory agencies can enhance the role of regulation in minimising market failures, by enabling regulatory agencies to address:

- **Lack of commitment, time inconsistency and political uncertainty:**
    - An independent regulator can *resist pressures to lower or increase prices at the expense of cost recovery, long-term maintenance and service quality* in the regulated sector;
    - A *long-term mandate of the regulator (beyond the electoral cycle, for example)* can help resolve time inconsistency and fluctuations linked to the political as well as economic business cycles.

- **Lack of competitive neutrality ensuring a level-playing field for all operators:**
    - An independent regulator signals to investors that the *rules will be set and followed without interference from the government*, and without undue preferential treatment linked to state ownership of certain market actors.

- **Information and expertise asymmetries:**
  - Independence promotes professionalism and expertise when the selection of staff (both senior management and professional) is based on merit. A regulator staffed with technical experts and shielded from political interference should have the *competence and skills* to: set prices which accurately reflect and adapt to costs; and monitor and enforce quality standards that preserve incentives for long-term performance, while maximising efficiency and welfare.
  - An independent regular might be more inclined to consult a broader spectrum of the population to *get a diversity of opinions* before making any regulatory decisions.
- **Regulatory capture:**
  - *Financial autonomy* of the regulator would mean in principle that the regulator has adequate resources to carry out its duties. This can help minimise opportunities for capture by industry and other lobby groups, as well as by government. Lack of resources can impede the capacity of regulators to take informed independent decisions.

Determinants

Understanding fully the determinants of independence across different market contexts, however, remains relatively difficult. Academics have developed a number of indices to measure and assess the drivers of independence (Box 1.3).

Box 1.3. Independence indexes: most frequent dimensions

- Budget independence;
- Conditions for dismissal of the head of the regulatory agency;
- Appointment of members/head of the regulatory agency by parliament or the legislature;
- Accountability and reporting to executive, legislature, or representatives from regulated industry;
- Power to set tariffs or price-setting; and
- Power to review or approve contract terms between regulated entities or market actors).

The majority of these indices have been produced taking the telecommunications market as a reference, in part because regulatory independence has a longer history in this sector. This sector focus masks some sector-specific differences. The OECD Product Market Regulation (PMR)'s Regulatory Management (RM) indicators for sector regulators, developed with inputs from the NER and drawing on the *OECD Best Practice Principles on the Governance of Regulators* (OECD, 2014), seek to address this sector bias by providing a more granular approach to independence (Koske et al., 2016). In addition, the PMR-RM indicators make a clear distinction between independence, accountability and scope of action of regulators, which tend to be somewhat blurred in the academic literature (Box 1.4).

> **Box 1.4. Product Market Regulation's sector regulators: independence**
>
> **Instructions from the executive**
>
> - The regulator can receive instructions/guidance from the government regarding long-term strategy, work programme, individual cases, appeals.
> - Which body, other than a court, can overturn the decisions of the regulator?
> - Is the regulator an independent body and is its independence explicitly stated in the law?
>
> **Staff**
>
> - How is the majority of the staff recruited?
> - Which body has the legal authority to make the final appointment of the agency head/board members?
> - Are there restrictions regarding the employment history of the agency head/board members?
> - May the agency head/board members hold other offices/appointments in the government/the regulated industry?
> - How can the agency head/board members be dismissed from office?
> - Can the agency head/board members take jobs in government or regulated sector after their term of office?
> - How long is the term of office of the agency head/board members?
>
> **Budget**
>
> - How is the regulator financed?
>
> *Source*: OECD (2016b), "Indicators of Product Market Regulation Homepage", www.oecd.org/economy/growth/indicatorsofproductmarketregulationhomepage.htm (accessed 15 April 2016).

The PMR-RM indicators, like most of the indexes developed by academics, focus on *de jure* formal requirements for independence. Yet a regulator can be part of a ministry and in fact be more "independent" than a regulator that is a separate body. Studies and surveys conducted by transnational networks of sector regulators have stressed the importance of the financial autonomy of regulators as a key practical determinant of independence. This attention for this practical aspect of independence partly reflect EU legislation in the energy and telecommunications sectors, which prescribes some form of autonomy for national regulatory authorities to manage their budget. Nevertheless, with the exception of these few surveys, attempts to capture *de facto* regulatory independence have been few. Some examples include measuring time-sensitive political variability, mostly based on leadership turnover in regulatory agencies. These attempts have been mostly focused on the telecommunications sector.

Outcomes

Independence is a means to an end: if regulatory independence truly provides a solution to market failures, the results should be visible in terms of improved market outcomes. Some econometric studies have used independence as an explanatory variable to investigate the determinants of, among others: efficiency and performance in the regulated sector; infrastructure quality and coverage in the sector; or consumer prices. At the micro-economic level, effects on levels of firm investment, as well as leverage of the incumbent, have been analysed. In general, revenue stability and investor certainty (rather than predictability) are viewed as important elements which regulators can bring to markets. In part due to methodological constraints, few authors have so far assessed the counter-factual: for example, to what extent private investment may be crowded out, or the market share of incumbent operators increased, in the absence of independent regulation.

Overall, due to the frequently binary nature of the regulatory independence measure in most studies, and /or to the variety of other much broader governance variables included in the analysis (such as generic rule of law measures), it is very difficult to pinpoint the effect of independence itself on these macro- and micro-economic outcomes. Few attempts have been made to isolate the effect of any specific feature of independence.

The how of independence

There have been few attempts to unpack some of the practical implications and features of independence and how these features are practiced by regulators. The independence survey conducted among NER members fills this gap. The analysis of the survey responses (presented in Chapter 3) points to some insights on the practical implications of the requirements and practices currently in place to safeguard independence:

Instructions from the executive

- **In some cases, executives issue statement of expectations and in a few cases, regulators respond with formal statements of intent to clarify how they plan to meet these expectations.** This process brings a certain degree of formality, as well as integrity and credibility to the relationship between the regulator and the executive and could potentially help resolve potential conflicts or misunderstandings between the regulator and the executive. The way in which these statements are delivered and their content can be particularly important. If the statements provide guidance on the direction of the regulatory activities, they can potentially bring clarity to the respective roles of the regulator and the executive and serve as an incentive to strengthen and improve internal processes (for example by providing guidance on better regulation policies or clarifying performance indicators). They could have little use if the statements become a "shopping list" of vague and broad expectations. They could end up being counterproductive if they are perceived as heavy handed, suggesting outcomes on technical areas which are clearly within the scope of the regulator's functions.

- **There are certain instances where the lack of clarity on roles and functions can open the door to undue government interventions.** Some regulators have been proactive in signalling these issues. In other cases, the deadlock has become evident and has been solved by a government intervention sometimes in conflict with the regulator. These instances can be disruptive for the regulatory environment, create uncertainty for investors and market operators on who is ultimately in charge of supervising the sector. Some degree of overlapping is inevitable and intrinsic to the relationship between the executives and the regulators. However, confusion should be avoided, in order to minimise opportunities for deadlock. For instance, confusion could be dispelled and deadlocks could be prevented, by laying out in advance possible problematic areas and having regular exchanges on how to find solutions, in accordance with the legitimate and appropriate roles and responsibilities.

- **The legislative process and parliament can prove useful in solving deadlocks created by lack of clarity on the boundaries between regulators and governments.** Grey areas will inevitably remain as it is challenging to set clear roles and boundaries between the responsibilities of the executive and those of the regulator. Dialogue and regular exchange of information between regulators and parliament can inform parliamentarians on the role of regulators and facilitate an informed debate when issues emerge.

- **The use of public consultations in the development of policies, laws, and regulations can help regulators obtain and disclose the views of the executive in a transparent way. Yet, the government or industry could also be heavy handed and try to hijack the process.** Informal and regular exchange of information could also be an effective way of complementing more formal channels of communication. However, there must be clarity in making exchanges transparent when appropriate, for instance through guidelines on legal obligations from, for example, "Freedom of Information" or "Public Ethics and Behaviour" rules and standards.

- **Media statements go beyond the usual institutional channels and can become a solution of "last resort" either to exercise some influence on regulators or to respond to attempts by government to unduly influence the work of the regulator.** They seem to be used with some care by government and regulators but used nevertheless. The media can serve as a useful, transparent reminder of the respective roles of the regulator and the executive (and in some instances the media have been relied upon for this purpose). However, the media can also have their own biases and, in the absence of a pluralistic media landscape, their useful role can be seriously diminished.

- **Some regulators have been proactive in scanning the horizon of the markets they oversee and signal potential emerging issues.** This proactivity has been sometimes perceived as an encroachment on the prerogatives of the executive. Yet, it can also provide precious advice to ministries and ultimately serve society. As noted above, some degree of overlapping is inevitable and "grey areas" are almost intrinsic to the work of regulators as it is not always easy to clearly define where role of the regulator ends and policy setting by elected officials start. In certain instances, it might be more appropriate for the regulator to signal issues that need to be taken into consideration by policy makers in advance to ministries before going public. Circumstances where ministries lack the political or administrative capacity to undertake this important function, regulators should be enabled with a legitimate mechanism to provide strategic foresight.

Relationship with industry and other non-government stakeholders

- **Regulators have developed a wide range of consultative tools to interact with industry and collect their inputs during the preparation of the regulatory decisions. Some regulators have also set up advisory bodies composed of industry representatives to institutionalise consultation.** Transparency and consultation can be an effective way of ensuring that decisions build on a wide range of evidence and are perceived as reflecting the needs and the legitimate demands of industry and users.

- **More problematic are those cases where stakeholders (especially industry) can exercise pressures on ministers and members of parliament to affect the decisions of the regulator. The effectiveness of these pressures can depend to a large extent on the degree to which the regulator is protected from (undue) pressures from the executive and parliament.** However, elected governments are ultimately responsible for determining the mandate and powers of regulators and these interventions can ultimately impact the power and role of the regulator.

- **Consultation can also be hijacked by powerful lobby groups that can delay or block decisions that go against their interest (but not necessarily against the collective/public interest).** In these cases, transparency and consultation could undermine or curtail rather than strengthen the regulators' independence.

- **Consultation can also become erroneously conflated in the public's mind with consensus. Mixing up consultation with negotiation can create unrealistic expectations on the extent to which the broad range of stakeholder views can be reflected in the final decision.** Informed participation by stakeholders could help dispel some of these confusions. Informed participation might be facilitated by providing clear and simplified information on the issues at stake and proactively reaching out to those stakeholders who can be less resourceful like residential consumers or new market entrants. Holding multilateral and bilateral discussions before public consultation can also be a means of placing all stakeholders on a level playing field, setting the ground rules for consultation, and identifying critical questions on which stakeholder input should be solicited. Clear timelines for consultation could also assist regulators so as to avoid prolonged or untimely interference (as well as deadlock) in the decision-making process.

- **There should be a balance between having accountability for regulatory decisions and "gaming" of the regulatory process so that decisions are made in the best interests of citizens.** Some consultations can be very technical and only of interest to few interested parties. In such cases innovative processes should be developed that enable regulators to conduct due diligence without wasting resources. These processes should be compatible with the relevant legal obligations should an appeal by an interested party be made to the judiciary.

- **Beyond formal consultations, stakeholders can try to influence regulators' decisions through lobbying targeting directly the regulator and, more indirectly, through lobbying or informal contacts with ministers and members of parliament.** Regulators have been relying on lobbying rules like obligations to register lobbyists and meeting with lobbyists to make the relationship with industry more transparent. More problematic are those cases where stakeholders (especially industry) can exercise pressures on ministers and members of parliament to affect the decisions of the regulator. The effectiveness of these pressures can depend to a large extent on the degree to which the regulator is protected from undue pressures from the executive and parliament. Some regulators have in part counteracted these pressures by going public on these issues and stirring at least a public debate among the citizens to whom governments are accountable.

Staff

Professionals

- **The way in which the regulators attract, retain and motivate staff is ultimately a key determinant of the capability of the regulator to *act* independently and take decisions that are objective and evidence-based.** Beyond the level of remuneration, that can be an issue in retaining senior level staff and more acute for some regulators, a number of regulators appear to have made a clear effort to create a culture of professionalism that provides a stronger guarantee of independence. This seems to have been achieved in part by inheriting public service values (including codes of conduct and procedures) and also a clear distinction between board (inevitably more political) and the professional body. This culture of professionalism accompanied by attention for "soft" incentives like having responsibility for making real impact, career progression, work-life balance and professional development appear to have in part compensated for the inevitable remuneration gap with the industry.

- **A number of regulators have conflict of interest policies and cooling-off periods for staff leaving the organisation. These policies appear to signal a clear and useful distinction between the regulator and the regulated industry.** Some of these policies often apply to the whole public sector and they appear to be relatively "light touch" (cooling-off periods tend to be in place mostly for senior professional staff). This is not necessarily an issue especially for more junior staff as some "back and forth" between the industry and the regulator can be mutually beneficial and provide useful exchanges of knowledge and skills.

Board/agency head

- **Board and agency heads are inevitably under more pressure from government and industry as they are ultimately responsible for the regulator's decisions. Accordingly, safeguards and protection from meddling and pressure is paramount. The nomination process (rather than the appointment) seems to be the crucial juncture.** The appointment of the regulator's head and/or board members is relatively transparent and can include checks and balances like parliamentary hearings and debates (with or without a formal vote). Yet, the process that leads to the choice of the nominees is in certain instances more of a "black box", where the proximity with the nominating authority or some "horse trading" deal could be perceived as more important than professionalism and objectivity. In some countries, the nominating authority – usually the executive – relies on independent search committees that could help in part open the black box and dispel these perceptions.

- **Most board members/agency heads are subject to cooling-off periods after leaving their position of 2 to 3 years in most cases.** Cooling-off periods can contribute to **signalling and promoting a culture of independence** and mark a clear boundary between industry and the regulator. However, they can also create **perverse incentives** in limiting the attractiveness of positions for experienced industry experts (or limiting the pool to end-of-career experts) and attract civil servants (who could potentially return to their positions but could also be more prone to pressures from the executive). Some of these perverse incentives can be minimised by having some compensation during the cooling-off period, which is the case for some regulators.

Budget

- **Source of funding – fees, general revenues or a mix of the two – vary but the source appear less important than the way in which funding needs are determined, appropriated and ultimately spent to determine the extent to which regulators can *act* independently.** Regardless of the source of funding, most regulators' budgets are part of the national budget. Far from being an encroachment on their independence, this appears to be a guarantee of transparency and accountability of regulators to citizens that can strengthen (rather than undermine) their independence.

- **For regulators funded through fees, an appropriate cost-recovery mechanism appear to be essential to set the "right" fee and avoid having a regulator that is under-funded or captured either by industry or undermined by the executive (for example in countries with still large regulated state-owned enterprises).** For most regulators, the fee is set by the executive within a legislated ceiling. This could be problematic especially in those countries where the government has large shares in some of the regulated companies. Some regulators have set up advisory committees composed by regulator and industry officials to review cost estimates.

- **For regulators funded through general revenues, it can be easier to influence the regulator by reducing the resources at the disposal of the regulator especially if the executive or parliament is not satisfied with a decision taken by regulator.** Annual appropriations can make it easier to influence the regulator than multi-annual appropriations that are less contingent to short-term political/electoral imperatives. Adequate safeguards should be provided so that the budget process does not become a tool to unduly direct the regulator.

References

Koske, I., et al. (2016), "Regulatory management practices in OECD countries", *OECD Economics Department Working Papers*, No. 1296, OECD Publishing, Paris. http://dx.doi.org/10.1787/5jm0qwm7825h-en.

OECD (2016a), "The OECD Network of Economic Regulators", www.oecd.org/gov/regulatory-policy/ner.htm (accessed 15 April 2016).

OECD (2016b), "Indicators of Product Market Regulation Homepage", http://www.oecd.org/economy/growth/indicatorsofproductmarketregulationhomepage.htm (accessed 15 April 2016).

OECD (2015), OECD Survey on the independence of economic regulators.

OECD (2014), *The Governance of Regulators*, OECD Best Practice Principles for Regulatory Policy, OECD Publishing, Paris, http://dx.doi.org/10.1787/9789264209015-en.

Chapter 2

Why does independence matter? The view from the literature

Independence is a means towards more effective outcomes rather than an end in itself. As a variety of pressures are put on regulators and independence of regulators becomes a question of increasing debate, it is particularly important to identify what is the value added of independence. Drawing on a review of the literature, this chapter describes the determinants of independence and the expected outcomes of independence.

Rationale for independence

A variety of pressures are placed on regulators, making their level of independence a question of increasing debate. Evolutions in information technology are making the environment within which they operate more dynamic and susceptible to rapid change. In addition, the post-financial crisis world has led to greater scrutiny of financial regulators in particular. Infrastructure regulators have not been spared, in a context of volatility in energy markets and pressures on delivery of basic utilities (especially in countries with continued strong demographic and industrial growth, but not only). Independence of regulators is thus being placed increasingly prominently on the political agenda. This includes not only independence from government and politicians, but also from firms in the regulated sectors, as well as other interest groups (e.g. consumer and environmental groups).

The OECD *Best Practice Principles on the Governance of Regulators* (OECD, 2014) recognise that establishing the regulator with a degree of independence (both from those it regulates and from government) can provide greater confidence and trust that regulatory decisions are made with integrity. Independent regulatory decision making, at arm's length from the political process, is likely to be especially important where both government and non-government entities are regulated under the same framework and competitive neutrality is therefore required. Independence is also crucial where the decisions of the regulator can have a significant impact on particular interests (such as industry), and there is a therefore need to protect its impartiality. These conditions are prevalent in infrastructure markets, as well as in the financial sector.

Historically, independent regulators have emerged over time in sectors where performance needed to be incentivised over a long term period (maintenance of long-term assets for instance, such as rail); and/ or where there was a need for new investment (advocacy for privatisation by an independent regulator could for instance help make such changes more palatable to the public). In some cases because of this historical/ context specificity, regulation was intended to be merely an interim measure which would disappear as competition flourished. However, regulators have remained very present in multiple markets. The political rationale has thus been twofold: protecting consumers and attracting investment on efficient terms; as well as helping mitigate political risk perceived by private investors.

Independence is a tool towards more effective outcomes – and not an end in itself. To ensure that independence is accurately understood and delivers the expected results, it is worth scanning the literature to identify precisely which challenges independence is expected (or assumed) to address. This can also help bridge the gap between formal (*de jure*) independence and practical (*de facto*) independence – so as to highlight more specifically what value-added or solution the regulator brings to the market. Economic theory pictures the role of regulation as a remedy (or 'second-best solution') to market failure or other related failure. Regulation is intended to mitigate these failures, at minimum cost – that is, without resulting in policy failures and excessive market distortions. Drawing on a recent literature review of the topic (Zhelyazkova, 2016a), Table 2.1 provides a classification of typical failures in regulated industries, together with the means through which regulatory independence, according to the literature, is expected to help.

Table 2.1. **Theoretical (market failure) arguments for regulatory independence**

Type of market failure	Description	Relevance of independent regulation	Caveats / sector specificities
Externalities and lack of commitment/ time Inconsistency/ political uncertainty Examples in the literature: Waverman and Koutroumpis (2011); Gilardi (2005a, b); Majone (1996); Armstrong and Sappington (2007); Murillo and Post (2014)	The market will not efficiently clear because of externalities: the marginal social benefit of the infrastructure (that is, the additional social welfare from one more unit of infrastructure produced or maintained) is higher than the marginal private benefit, or what consumers are each willing to pay for their use of the good. This means that the externality cannot be reasonably reflected in the price of the service, if consumers are to keep purchasing it. Moreover although social efficiency would require setting prices should at the marginal cost, prices must at least equal the average cost for long-term financial viability. Regulation or government action is therefore needed to set tariffs. However the tariff setting function can suffer from political (or industry) pressure. The government can have an incentive to reduce prices after a firm has made an investment in the sector (classic "hold-up problem" because the capital costs are high, up-front, and result in sunk immoveable assets; as a result the investor is not foot-loose and must remain in business even if infrastructure tariffs are reduced for populist motives). The government can decide to change	The regulator is not dependent on the government and can resist the pressure from users. It has no direct incentives to lower prices in favour of users at the expense of revenue recovery for firms operating in the regulated sector. The regulator is appointed with a long-term mandate, which can help resolve time inconsistency and political business cycle fluctuations by sending the signal that its policies will be long-term as well. The tariff structure and how it is set by regulators can have indirect effects on incentives and resources for quality and upkeep of infrastructure assets over the long-term.	Independence provides a solution only for "indirect expropriation" (i.e. de facto expropriation of the asset by modifying the revenue flows that the firm can expect from it); but it does not address the more fundamental risk of direct expropriation which is also contained in the "hold-up problem". More fundamentally, the "hold-up" theory is only relevant as long as the investment is a "one-time game". In a repeated game situation with recurrent investments, there would be little reason for agents (including government) to modify their behaviour before and after the investment). The relation to time is double-edged for regulators: on the one hand, stability can

Table 2.1. **Theoretical (market failure) arguments for regulatory independence** (*cont.*)

Type of market failure	Description	Relevance of independent regulation	Caveats / sector specificities
	policy (e.g. because of election), which could impact significantly on the business in the regulated sector. Firms therefore under-invest in the sector. Not just governments, but investors and regulated entities as well, can adopt short-term views. In infrastructure sectors this can be the detriment of network quality, innovation, replacement, and maintenance. If tariffs do not cover the long-term depreciation of capital assets for instance, very short-sighted investment decisions may result.		reassure market actors (especially when political decisions are taken on a shorter timeframe); but alongside, the regulator is expected preserve flexibility and adapt to short-term sector specificities.
Lack of competitive neutrality (competition with public firms, or with private monopolies) Examples in the literature: Edwards and Waverman (2006); Gonenc et al.(2000)	Due to asset specificity and economies of scope and scale (especially in infrastructure sectors), natural (public or private) monopolies can arise. In these cases the optimal price for the monopolist, which is set so as to maximise the monopolist's revenue, seldom matches the social optimal (which would be at the marginal cost of production). If liberalisation has occurred prior to privatisation or if the government is the main shareholder of the incumbent, potential entrants may hesitate to invest in a sector where the government will have a conflict of interest as both owner and regulator.	The establishment of an independent regulator sends the signal to investors that the rules will be set and followed without interference by the government. In particular it helps create an assurance of a "level playing field", whereby market competitors will not benefit from undue advantages or preferential treatment in light of their state-owned status.	The level of asset specificity and economies of scope and scale will differ across markets. Independent regulation alone may not improve the corporate governance of state-owned enterprises in the market (which can pose an equally strong constraint on market outcomes).
Information asymmetry (and resulting moral hazard as well as adverse selection) Examples in the literature: Laffont and Tirole (1986); Bawn (1995)	The regulated firms (the agents) usually know better than the government (the principal) what their operating costs and profitable margins are. And even when the realised production costs can be observed by the regulator, the same cannot be said of how much effort the firm has put into cost-reduction (a post-contractual hidden effort problem, as summarised by the seminal work of Laffont and Tirole, 1986). Moreover, the firm knows more about its cost-reducing technology than the regulator (a pre-contractual hidden information problem). Not only does this make it	If the regulatory agency is managed by experts in the regulated field, it should have the technical competence to set prices and determine entry and exit criteria, as well as to monitor and enforce performance and quality standards. This requires very sector-specific knowledge: as illustrated by Laffont and Tirole (2000), although general theories can be of great	In practice, sector regulators seldom have the capacity and real-time information to overcome these asymmetries (both pre-contractual hidden information, and post-contractual hidden effort). There is a particular challenge for setting prices and monitoring behaviour while preserving space for long-term innovation and resilience by

Table 2.1. **Theoretical (market failure) arguments for regulatory independence** (*cont.*)

Type of market failure	Description	Relevance of independent regulation	Caveats / sector specificities
	more difficult to accurately set tariffs; it can also generate moral hazard (if regulated firms conceal the underlying state of infrastructure assets and take the risk of under-maintaining them) as well as adverse selection (firms that spend more in infrastructure maintenance will be "costed out" of the market).	value, in the end all regulation must be industry-specific.	regulated entities.
Private capture/ lobbying Examples in the literature: Stigler (1971); Dal Bó (2006)	If the government is regulating the sector it can become "captured" by the industry and advance their interests to the detriment of consumers.	An independent regulator with own financing can address this problem. The distinction between political and managerial autonomy (Andres et al., 2007); and/ or between statutory and functional independence (Mohammed and Strobl, 2011) is relevant here.	The regulating agency can also become captured by powerful consumers (big multinationals, etc.).

Source: Expanded from Zhelyazkova, N. (2016a), "The Independence of Regulatory Agencies in Network Industries: Literature Review", *Working Paper of the Chair of Governance and Regulation*, Dauphine University, Paris, forthcoming.

Determinants of independence

A better understanding of the ways in which independence is expected to work can help countries develop and maintain a culture of independence, and can also suggest in which sectors or contexts such independence is more or less feasible or desirable. Several indices of independence have been built in the academic literature, in addition to the OECD indicators of Regulatory Management for regulators of network sectors as part of the OECD Product Market Regulation dataset (Koske et al., 2016).

The dimensions of regulatory independence thus analysed frequently fall into two broad categories: one more related to the political or institutional set-up of the regulator; and the other to the structure and sources of its budget and the scope of its functions. As identified by Zhelyazkova (2016a), Andres et al. (2007) for instance distinguish between political autonomy and managerial autonomy, while Mohammed and Strobl (2011) define statutory and functional independence (the former consisting in operational separation from the executive, and the latter referring to the regulatory functions the regulator is authorised to perform).

While different authors have identified a wide range of different features of independence, there is in general quite a broad overlap or consensus across several dimensions. Table 2.2 compares the items used in indices of regulatory independence across five studies, informed by the synthesis work of Montoya and Trillas (2007) as well as Martin and Jayakar (2013). In cases where several of these dimensions or criteria address a similar topic (for instance, the term of office for directors and whether contracts of directors can be renewed), they have been grouped within a single category for better comparability. Relevant elements of the OECD Product Market Regulation's Regulatory Management (PMR-RM) indicators for sector regulators are also featured below.

Table 2.2. **Features of independence common to academic literature**

Feature of independence	Gual & Trillas (2006)	Edwards and Waverman (2006)	Gutiérrez (2003)	Waverman & Koutroumpis (2011)	Bauer (2003)	OECD PMR-RM indicators	Total
Budget and history							
1. Budget independence	x	x	x	x	x	x	6
Staff							
2. Can the head of the agency be dismissed?	x	x	x			x	4
3. Years since agency was established / is the agency older than two years?	x	x		x			3
4. Term of office for directors / can contracts of directors be renewed?	x	x				x	3
5. Appointment by parliament or government	x	x		x	x	x	5
6. Size (number of staff)		x					1
7. Restrictions regarding employment history of head/ board members						x	1
8. Holding by board members of other appointments in government/ industry						x	1

Table 2.2. **Features of independence common to academic literature** (*cont.*)

Feature of independence	Gual & Trillas (2006)	Edwards and Waverman (2006)	Gutiérrez (2003)	Waverman & Koutroumpis (2011)	Bauer (2003)	OECD PMR-RM indicators	Total
Working relationship with executive and accountability to public							
9. Reports to / directly accountable to executive, legislature, or representatives from regulated industry		x		x	x	x	4
10. Must make interconnection agreements public (prices, licenses, spectrum policy etc.)			x	x			2
11. Agency scope / shared power with executive	x	x			x		3
12. Can government overrule agency decision?					x	x*	2
13. Collegiate vs. individual office		x					1
14. Written / verbal instructions by the executive		x				x**	2
15. Mechanism to explain & publicise decisions/ report on activities			x			x***	2
Functions and powers in regulated market							
16. Power to set tariffs / prices set by executive	x		x	x	x	x	5
17. Share of public/private ownership of incumbent	x						1
18. Power to allocate licenses	x					x	2
19. Power to revoke, modify or suspend licenses				x			1
20. Power to allocate spectrum / power over an interconnection	x	x		x	x	x	5

Table 2.2. **Features of independence common to academic literature** (*cont.*)

Feature of independence	Gual & Trillas (2006)	Edwards and Waverman (2006)	Gutiérrez (2003)	Waverman & Koutroumpis (2011)	Bauer (2003)	OECD PMR-RM indicators	Total
21. Power to administer universal service	x						1
22. Creation & functions defined by law or lower legal text, or executive order			x			x	2
23. Are regulator and operator separated / year of separation mandated?			x		x		2
24. Mechanism to resolve / arbitrate disputes			x		x	x	3
25. Power to enforce fines			x	x		x	3

* The PMR question is broader and asks "which body, other than a court" can over-turn the regulator's decision (this thus potentially includes regulated entities as well).

** the PMR questions on instructions from the executive have some granularity, investigating whether these instructions pertain to: i) long term strategies, ii) work programmes, iii) individual cases or iv) decisions and appeals.

*** The PMR question on reporting by the regulator questions which performance information is provided: industry and market performance; operational/service delivery; organisational/corporate governance performance; quality of regulatory process; compliance with legal obligations; economic performance; and financial performance. It also asks whether this information is available on the internet, and whether the he costs of operating the regulator are published and accessible to the public.

Source: OECD (2014), *The Governance of Regulators*, OECD Best Practice Principles for Regulatory Policy, OECD Publishing, Paris, http://dx.doi.org/10.1787/9789264209015-en; Montoya, M.A. and F. Trillas (2007), "The measurement of the independence of telecommunications regulatory agencies in Latin America and the Caribbean", *Utilities Policy*, Vol. 15/3, pp. 182-190; Martin, B.L. and K. Jayakar (2013), "Moving beyond dichotomy: Comparing composite telecommunications regulatory governance indices", *Telecommunications Policy*, Vol. 37/9, pp. 691-701; Zhelyazkova, N. (2016a), "The Independence of Regulatory Agencies in Network Industries: Literature Review", *Working Paper of the Chair of Governance and Regulation*, Dauphine University, Paris, forthcoming;

Table 2.2 suggests that the most frequently used dimensions of regulatory independence are:

- Budget independence;
- Conditions for dismissal of the head of the regulatory agency;

- Appointment of members/head of the regulatory agency by parliament or the legislature;
- Accountability and reporting to executive, legislature, or representatives from regulated industry;
- Power to set tariffs or price-setting by the executive; and
- Power to review or approve contract terms between regulated entities or market actors).

These dimensions correspond to many of the measures of "formal independence" flagged by Gilardi and Maggetti (2010). They also map closely with the seven dimensions identified by Martin and Jayakar (2013) as most frequently used in an earlier synthesis of five of these studies (which did not include the OECD PMR-RM indicators). The two dimensions that are no longer prominent when the OECD PMR-RM indicators are added seem to be: regulatory functions shared with the executive; and length of operation of the regulator (often set at a minimum of two years). Interestingly, several of the dimensions in Table 2.1 which the literature has tended to use as measures of independence are in fact listed in the OECD PMR-RM indicators as measures of accountability (items 9 and 15 above) or of scope of action (16-20, 24 and 25). This may point to a blurring in the literature between the concept of independence strictly speaking, and other measures of regulatory quality.

Looking into the details, several of the OECD measures provide more granularity on specific features of regulatory governance: notably on the information reported by the regulator, on whether this information is available online, and on what types of instructions the regulator can receive from the executive (see notes to Table 2.1 above). Since the answers to these questions actually may not all have the same direction of relationship with independence, making such distinctions can be very useful. For instance according to the *OECD Best Practice Principles on the Governance of Regulators*, regulators should have sufficient autonomy to conduct their functions without interference from the executive, congress or parliament (this applies to work programmes, individual cases, and decisions and appeals). However, the long term strategy and policy goals of the regulator should be in line with the broad strategic national priorities as set by elected representatives in the executive, congress or parliament. While intervention of the executive in the former dimensions may negatively affect regulatory quality, in the latter case it may thus enhance it and allow to better close the regulatory policy cycle. Ignoring this type of nuance can lead to erroneously emphasising complete separation of the regulator from the executive and parliament, at the risk of breaking helpful feedback loops across the broader regulatory policy cycle.

Table 2.2 as well as the most recent literature review on the topic (Zhelyazkova, 2016a) suggest several additional gaps in terms of accurately understanding the determinants of regulatory independence. First, the majority of the literature and composite indices covered above have focused on the telecommunications market, in part because regulatory independence has a longer history in this sector for many countries, and also because private investment trends have generally been strongest here. This sector focus necessarily masks sector-specific differences. In fact as recognised by the OECD *Best Practice Principles on the Governance of Regulators*, the appropriate governance structure for market regulation "in each case will depend on the nature of the regulatory task and the sectors subject to the regulation". The same degree of independence (or, going further into the nuances of what constitutes independence, the same *type* of independence) may not be appropriate across all economic sectors and country contexts.

This type of nuance is particularly important in a context where multi-sector regulators are on the rise: two-thirds of the 34 water regulators reviewed by the OECD are for instance multi-sector bodies, and for the majority of these (20 out of 23), water is bundled with energy competencies (OECD, 2015). In some countries these multi-sector regulators are additionally merged with competition authorities or consumer agencies, as is the case with, most recently, Spain's National Authority for Markets and Competition (*Comisión Nacional de los Mercados y de la Competencia*, CNMC). This may be relevant to the study of independence, particularly if there are reasons to believe that competition and multi-sector authorities may be less prone to capture than single-sector regulators (for instance because they tend to deal with a much larger range of firms and consumers; or because, unlike in infrastructure sectors, there is no former incumbent in which the state is likely to be keeping an interest).

One of the most common areas of discussion in the literature includes measuring the *de jure* versus *de facto* aspects of regulatory independence. A regulator can be part of a ministry and yet be more "independent" than a regulator that is a separate body (OECD, 2014). Attempts to capture *de facto* regulatory independence have been few, but tend to be more dynamic in nature. As identified by Zhelyazkova (2016a), Cukierman and Webb (1995) assess the probability of a change in leadership of the central bank following a change in government power; and Trillas and Montoya (2008) apply a similar logic to the telecommunications sector (in particular, the turnover in the direction of the regulator, and how soon after a change in government the head of an agency is also changed). A version of the time-varying political variability or "vulnerability index" calculated by Trillas (2010) for telecommunications regulators could have interesting applications for other sectors which may be even more vulnerable to political pressure, such as water or energy. Other measures of *de facto* independence suggested by Gilardi and Maggetti (2010) include the frequency of contacts with politicians and regulates, the partisanship of nominations, and the professional activity of the chairperson or board members. Going further, such measures could perhaps usefully consider not only changes at the head of the regulatory agency, but also less visible changes such as the evolution of tariff levels in relationship to the political business cycle.

A number of recent academic publications have suggested that participation of regulators in regulatory networks operating across sectors and national borders can enhance the independence of regulators (Zhelyazkova, 2016b). In particular, Bach and Ruffing (2013) have developed an analytical framework for explaining the effect of EU-involvement on the autonomy of agencies. As a possible mechanism the authors suggests that network membership can enhance autonomy by providing access to important knowledge to network members. Through network participation, regulators could gain greater levels of expertise in their field of operation, including knowledge on potential solutions regulators could propose to the government using also information on what is achievable at the international level.

Transnational networks of sector regulators have also facilitated discussion and analysis of the status of independence among their members, relying in part on indexes developed by academics (Zhelyazkova, 2016b). For example, 26 members of the Energy Regulators Regional Association (ERRA) were surveyed in 2014-15 on the formal dimensions of independence identified by Gilardi (2005a). Respondents highlighted the importance of financial independence in order to guarantee that there are adequate human resources and an appropriate working environment for efficient operation and predictable, consistent and un-biased decisions (ERRA, 2015). In 2014, the European Platform of Regulatory Agencies (EPRA), which brings together 52 European broadcasting regulators, conducted a survey of its members focussing on the perceptions that regulatory agencies have of their own independence and the practices they use to safeguard their independence. Similarly to the results of the ERRA survey, the majority of the 26 respondents indicated that management of financial and human resources are key prerequisites for independence (EPRA, 2014). In 2014, the European Regulators Group for Audio-Visual Media Services (ERGA) also surveyed 33 European audio-visual regulators on a number of key dimensions of independence, including appointment of board members, human resources, financial autonomy, accountability and transparency, and enforcement. Findings of the survey highlight the importance of autonomy in preparing and allocating the budget, as well as some degree of autonomy in enforcing decisions to guarantee independence (ERGA, 2015).

The focus of European networks on independence reflects in part the existence of EU legislation providing for the establishment of independent regulatory authorities in some network sectors (Zhelyazkova, 2016c). For the electricity and gas sectors, EU directives contain specific provisions on budget, human resources and appointment of management to guarantee that regulatory authorities are "legally and functionally independent from other public or private entities."[1] For the telecommunications sector, the directive requires the establishment of provisions that protect the regulator against "external intervention and political pressure."[2] In particular, on financial autonomy, the electricity and gas directives provide for separate annual budget allocations, with autonomy in the implementation of the allocated budget, in addition to adequate human and financial resources to carry out these duties. The telecom directive refers to the need for the regulatory authority to have its own budget allowing the authority to recruit a sufficient number of qualified staff. These provisions are less detailed in the case of the airport charges directive which requires member states to guarantee the legal and functional independence of the supervisory authority from any airport managing body and air carrier.[3]

Outcomes of independence

A survey of the literature on independence can also be useful because it gives an insight on the various expected (and actual) outcomes of regulation – corresponding to the idea of independence being a means to an end, and not an end in itself. In this perspective, independence has been used as an explanatory variable – whether in binary form or as a composite index – for econometric studies investigating the determinants of a range of outcomes, including: efficiency and performance in the regulated sector; infrastructure coverage in the sector; or prices faced by consumers (Zhelyazkova, 2016a). Yet more nuance is often needed across these dimensions: for instance, it may be useful not just to consider whether consumer prices have gone up or down – but rather whether the price better reflects efficient costs, and makes for a better value proposition for consumers, as a result of independence.

Meanwhile at the micro-economic level, effects on levels of firm investment, as well as leverage of the incumbent, have been analysed. In general revenue stability and investor certainty (rather than predictability) is viewed as an important element which regulators can bring to markets. In this context it might also be useful to assess the counter-factual, which few authors have done in part due to methodological constraints: for example, to what extent private investment may be crowded out, or the market share of incumbent operators increased, in the absence of independent regulation.

It is becoming increasingly important to verify the validity of these links, as in some cases (the positive relationship with private investment flows for instance) they are readily assumed by actors such as credit rating agencies or superannuation groups, which may factor regulatory independence into their assessment of country and sector investment grades. Meanwhile more indirect effects of regulatory independence, for instance the possible impact on incentives for innovation or long-term investments in infrastructure maintenance by regulated entities, appear to have seldom been considered.

Political economy arguments have also explored how regulation might affect the regulated entity's strategic behaviour. For instance the operator may demonstrate higher leverage in the hopes that the regulator, due to fear for the operator's financial viability, will increase tariffs and thus the operator's cost recovery prospects as a result (Spiegel and Spulber, 1994; Bortolotti et al., 2011). The direction of causality for this type of strategic argument can of course also be reversed: Gual and Trillas (2003) for instance find that markets with larger incumbents tend to have more independent agencies, and posit that this may be because larger incumbents might feel that regulators that are independent from the government would be easier to co-opt. Moreover, within the framework of interest group pressure, larger incumbents and the state typically have huge sunk investments in infrastructure and may be more cautious of potential losses from underinvestment in the absence of an independent regulator.

Overall, due to the frequently binary nature of the regulatory independence measure, and /or to the variety of other much broader governance variables included in the analysis (such as generic rule of law measures), it is very difficult to pinpoint the effect of independence itself on these macro- and micro-economic outcomes. This might especially be complicated by the fact that, as has been pointed out by the NER in the past, independence is often a "necessary but not sufficient" condition for regulatory quality in a sector. In fact as the blurred line between measures of independence and accountability illustrated earlier in Table 2.2, regulators are very rarely independent without also being relatively accountable and having an effective scope of action. Separating these different dimensions can be rather difficult in practice, and doing so might actually have limited meaning when attempting to identify the impacts on regulated sectors.

Even when more complex measures of independence are used (such as composite indices which may contain the many variables illustrated in Table 2.2), few attempts have been made to isolate the effect of any specific feature of this independence. Yet not all features go hand-in-hand, and some may in fact have countervailing effects depending on the market context. Whichever measure of independence is used, the classic challenges of omitted variable bias, reverse causality and measurement error also inevitably arise. It has been difficult to find econometric solutions to overcome these – in particular, few variables have been found to be meet the twin conditions of relevance and exogeneity, so as to qualify as econometric "instruments" for independence (Zhelyazkova, 2016a). Moreover randomised control trials or quasi-experiments (which may be the most effective way of capturing *de facto* independence, for instance via interrupted time series analysis) have seldom been conducted as they may require a longer time-series and a higher frequency of regulatory changes in order to provide any useful conclusions.

Nevertheless, even in this context of severe methodological constraints, economic regulators collect a wealth of information that is highly sector-specific and which could be much better utilised for analysis as well as benchmarking – to better understand both the determinants of independence, and its outcomes. Further practical and theoretical analysis could in particular shed light on the channels leading from different features of independence, to different market (macro- and micro-economic) outcomes, including on:

- the types of variables which could more usefully be included in any composite indices of regulatory independence;
- which features or types of independence are better suited to which market contexts;
- the likely outcomes of independence on regulated markets, both direct and indirect (such as on innovation), and differentiated by sector; and
- the specific transmission channels through which these effects might operate.

Notes

1. Directive 2009/72/EC, Chapter IX, Art. 35 (electricity); Directive 2009/73/EC, Chapter VIII, Art. 39 (gas).
2. Directive 2009/140/EC, Art. 13.
3. Directive 2009/12/EC.

References

Andres, L. et al. (2007), "Assessing the Governance of Electricity Regulatory Agencies in the Latin American and Caribbean Region : A Benchmarking Analysis", *Policy Research Working Paper 4380*, November.

Armstrong, M. and D.E. Sappington (2007), "Recent Developments in the Theory of Regulation", in Armstrong, M. and R. Porter (eds.), *Handbook of Industrial Organization (Vol. III)*, pp. 1557-1700, Elsevier Science Publishers, Amsterdam.

Bach, T. and E. Ruffing (2013), "Networking for Autonomy? National Agencies in European Networks", *Public Administration*, Vol. 91/3, pp. 712-726.

Bauer, J.M. (2003), "The coexistence of regulation, state ownership and competition in infrastructure industries", *Quello Center Working Paper*, No. 03-03, Quello center for telecommunications management and law, Michigan state university, http://papers.ssrn.com/sol3/papers.cfm?abstract_id=397060 (accessed May 2016).

Bawn, K. (1995), "Political Control Versus Expertise: Congressional Choices about AdministrativeProcedures", *American Political Science Review*, Vol. 89/1, pp. 62-73.

Bortolotti, B. et al. (2011), "Capital Structure and Regulation: Do Ownership and Regulatory Independence Matter?", *Journal of Economics and Management Strategy*, Vol. 20/2, pp. 517-564.

Cukierman, A. and S. Webb (1995), "Political Influence on the Central Bank: International Evidence", *World Bank Economic Review*, Vol. 9/3, http://wber.oxfordjournals.org/content/9/3/397.short.

Dal Bo, E. (2006), "Regulatory Capture: A Review", *Oxford Review of Economic Policy*, Vol. 22/2, pp. 203-225.

Edwards, G. and L. Waverman (2006), "The Effects of Public Ownership and Regulatory Independence on Regulatory Outcomes", *Journal of Regulatory Economics*, Vol. 29/1, pp. 23-67.

Gilardi, F. (2005a), "The Formal Independence of Regulators: A Comparison of 17 Countries and 7 Sectors", *Swiss Political Science Review*, Vol. 11/4, pp. 139-167.

Gilardi, F. (2005b), "The Institutional Foundations of Regulatory Capitalism: The Diffusion of Independent Regulatory Agencies in Western Europe", *The ANNALS of the American Academy of Political and Social Science*, Vol. 598/1, pp. 84-101.

Gilardi, F. and M. Maggetti (2010), "The independence of regulatory authorities", in *Handbook of Regulation*, Eward Elgar, Cheltenham.

Gönenç, R., M. Maher and G. Nicoletti (2000), "The Implementation and the Effects of Regulatory Reform: Past Experience and Current Issues", *OECD Economics Department Working Papers*, No. 251, OECD Publishing, Paris, http://dx.doi.org/10.1787/413754754615.

Gual, J. and F. Trillas (2006), "Telecommunications Policies: Measurements and Determinants", *IESE Working Paper*, No. 630, IESE Business School, University of Navarra, Barcelona, May.

Gual, J. and F. Trillas (2003), "Telecommunications Policies: Determinants and Impact", *Working Paper*, 2003/2, Institut d'Economia de Barcelona (IEB).

Gutierrez, L.H. (2003), "The Effect of Endogenous Regulation on Telecommunications Expansion and Efficiency in Latin America", *Journal of Regulatory Economics*, Vol. 23/3, pp. 257-286.

Koske, I., et al. (2016), "Regulatory management practices in OECD countries", *OECD Economics Department Working Papers*, No. 1296, OECD Publishing, Paris, http://dx.doi.org/10.1787/5jm0qwm7825h-en.

Laffont, J.-J. and J. Tirole (1986), "Using cost observation to regulate firms", *Journal of Political Economy*, Vol. 94, pp. 614-641.

Majone, G. (1996), "Temporal Consistency and Policy Credibility: Why Democracies Need Non-Majoritarian Institutions", *EUI Working paper RSC*, Vol. 96/57, pp. 1-14.

Martin, B.L. and K. Jayakar (2013), "Moving beyond dichotomy: Comparing composite telecommunications regulatory governance indices", *Telecommunications Policy*, Vol. 37/9, pp. 691-701.

Mohammed, A.-M. and E. Strobl (2011), "Good Governance and Growth in Developing Countries: A Case Study of Regulatory Reforms in the Telecommunications Industry", *Journal of Industry, Competition and Trade*, Vol. 11/1, pp. 91-107.

Montoya, M.A. and F. Trillas (2007), "The measurement of the independence of telecommunications regulatory agencies in Latin America and the Caribbean", *Utilities Policy*, Vol. 15/3, pp. 182-190.

Murillo, M.V. and A. Post (2014), "Revisiting the Obsolescing Bargain in Post-Crisis Argentina: Investor Portfolios and Regulatory Outcomes", UC Berkeley and Columbia University.

OECD (2015), *The Governance of Water Regulators*, OECD Studies on Water, OECD Publishing, Paris, http://dx.doi.org/10.1787/9789264231092-en.

OECD (2014), *The Governance of Regulators*, OECD Best Practice Principles for Regulatory Policy, OECD Publishing, Paris, http://dx.doi.org/10.1787/9789264209015-en.

Spiegel, Y. and D.F. Spulber (1994), *The RAND Journal of Economics*, Vol. 25/3, Autumn, pp. 424-440, www.jstor.org/stable/2555770?seq=1#page_scan_tab_contents.

Stigler, G.J. (1971), The Theory of economic Regulation", *The Bell Journal of Economics and Management Science*, Vol. 2/1, pp. 3-21.

Trillas, F. (2010), "Independent Regulators: Theory, Evidence and Reform Proposals", *IESE Business School Working Paper*, WP-860, May.

Trillas, F. and M.A. Montoya (2008), "The Degree of Commitment to Regulator Independence: Measurement and Impact", *Working Paper Series Centro Asia Pacific*, www.ief.es/documentos/recursos/publicaciones/revistas/hac_pub/185_D egree.pdf.

Waverman, L. and P. Koutroumpis (2011), "Benchmarking telecoms regulation the Telecommunications Regulatory Governance Index (TRGI)", *Telecommunications Policy*, Vol. 35/5, pp. 450-468.

Zhelyazkova, N. (2016a), "The Independence of Regulatory Agencies in Network Industries: Literature Review", *Working Paper of the Chair of Governance and Regulation,* Dauphine University, Paris, forthcoming.

Zhelyazkova, N. (2016b), "How do regulatory networks contribute to regulatory independence?", *Working Paper of the Chair of Governance and Regulation,* Dauphine University, Paris, forthcoming

Zhelyazkova, N. (2016c), "Regulatory Independence in the European Union", *Working Paper of the Chair of Governance and Regulation,* Dauphine University, Paris, forthcoming.

Chapter 3

How does independence work in practice? Key trends and evidence

Attempts to analyse the practical implications of independence have been limited. The survey conducted among more 48 regulators from 26 countries fills this gap. Drawing on this survey, this chapter presents some of the features of independence and how these features are practiced by regulators, focusing on the relationship with government and industry, staff and budget.

Instructions from the executive

Regulators are not an island. Rather, they are part of the policy-making process writ large and are particularly engaged in policy implementation (Table 3.1).

Table 3.1. **The reported actors at each stage of the regulatory cycle**

Based on 24 respondents

	Number of countries reporting involvement of actors at the following stages			
	Stage 1: Set policy	Stage 2: Design	Stage 3: Implement/ enforce	Stage 4: Evaluate
Parliament	7	6	2	4
Government collectively (e.g. Cabinet or President)	19	6	4	6
Individual ministries acting within their policy areas	15	20	14	15
National government body co-ordinating or overseeing regulatory proposals	17	20	6	10
Regulators	3	9	17	9
Supreme Audit Institutions	0	0	0	5
Other (sub-national) tiers of government	4	7	7	5
Civil society (business, citizens, etc.)	3	8	0	3

The shaded cells show the stages of the policy cycle where the actors engage more prominently.

Note: The 24 respondents included Australia, Austria, Brazil, Chile, Denmark, Estonia, the European Commission, Germany, Ireland, Italy, Japan, Korea, Luxembourg, Mexico, New Zealand, Norway, Poland, Slovak Republic, Slovenia, Spain, Sweden, Switzerland, Turkey and the United Kingdom.

Source: OECD (2015b), *OECD Regulatory Policy Outlook 2015*, OECD Publishing, Paris, http://dx.doi.org/10.1787/9789264238770-en.

In this context, it is inevitable (and probably desirable) that executives and regulators interact in their daily work. Responses to the survey suggest that these interactions take place either formally or informally. While they can be initiated by the executives, it is usually a two-way relationship where the regulators can respond to the executive's formal and informal interventions (sometimes to resist them if the regulator considers that these interventions are outside the executive's authority).

Formal interactions can take the form of statements of expectations, submissions during public consultation phases of proposed regulation or regulatory decisions and official co-ordination meetings between sector ministries and the regulators. Informal interactions can happen through public statements in the media as well as working-level exchanges between sector ministries and/or other government agencies and regulators (Figure 3.1).

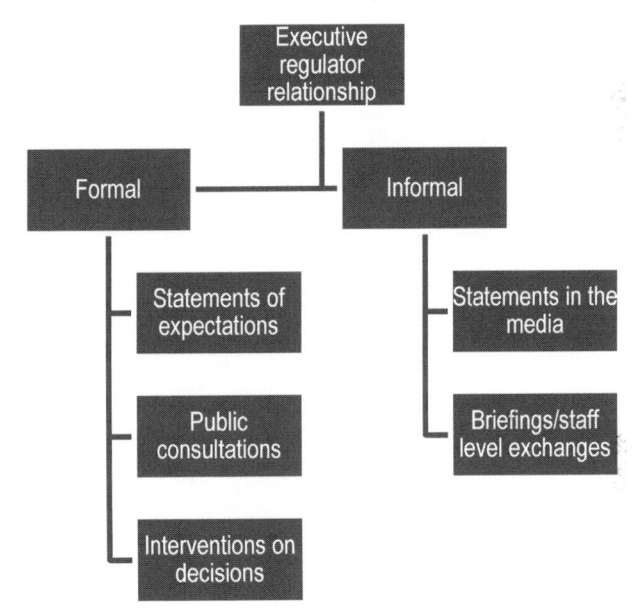

Figure 3.1. **Typology of interactions between executives and regulators**

```
                    Executive
                    regulator
                   relationship
                        |
         ┌──────────────┴──────────────┐
       Formal                        Informal
         │                              │
         ├── Statements of              ├── Statements in the
         │   expectations               │   media
         │                              │
         ├── Public                     └── Briefings/staff
         │   consultations                  level exchanges
         │
         └── Interventions on
             decisions
```

Source: Based on OECD (2015a), OECD Survey on the independence of economic regulators.

Stating expectations

Executives can issue statements on their expectations of how the regulator should conduct its activities. The degree of political interference with regulatory decisions would depend on how extensive the instructions are: whether they provide a loose policy framework within which the regulator has freedom to choose how it plans to meet those policy goals, or whether the government is present at every step of the regulatory process to direct the regulatory agenda. Twelve regulators are issued with some sort of expectation/policy statement, out of which 8 indicated that such statements are binding or influence their actions. These include Ofgem, Ofwat, the Water Industry Commission for Scotland, the Norwegian Communications Authority (Nkom), the Alberta Energy Regulator, the ACCC and the Australian Energy Regulator (Figure 3.2).

Figure 3.2. **Does the government issue formal statements on its expectations of the conduct of the regulator's activities?**

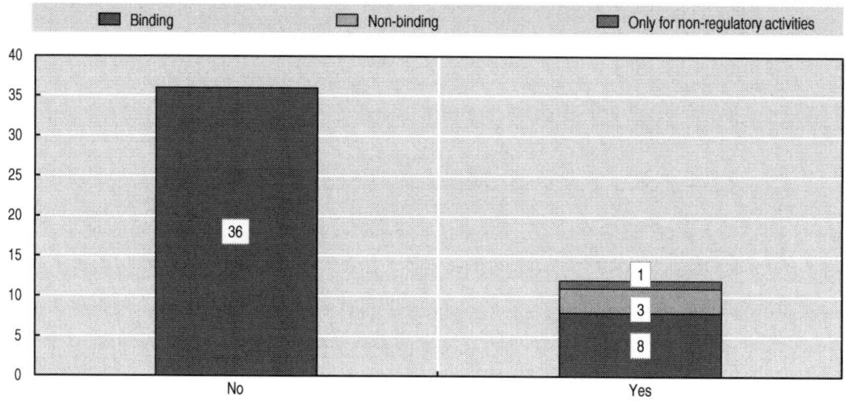

[Bar chart showing: No = 36 (Binding); Yes = 8 (Binding), 3 (Non-binding), 1 (Only for non-regulatory activities)]

Source: OECD (2015a), OECD Survey on the independence of economic regulators.

Three regulators – the Australian Competition and Consumer Commission (ACCC), the Australian Energy Regulator, and the Alberta Energy Regulator – respond to these statements with a statement of intent where the regulator outlines how it plans on meeting these expectations. The Essential Services Commission of South Australia (ESCOSA) included a Statement of Regulatory Intent in its Strategic Plan 2015-18 and plans to do so for the forthcoming revision of the Plan. While this statement is not a direct response to a specific policy statement from the Government, the Commission has adopted this approach to support a better regulation practice and culture within the organisation. In the case of the French Energy Regulatory Commission (*Commission de régulation de l'énergie*, CRE), the executive can only issue non-binding statements on specific regulatory activities (specified in the law) and binding statements on non-regulatory duties relating to the implementation of government policy.

Some of these statements of expectations are relatively short and lay out government expectations on process (e.g. use of better regulation tools and attention for administrative burden reduction) rather than on specific regulatory issues. This is the case for the ACCC and the Australian Energy Regulator (Box 3.1). The regulators in turn respond through a Statement of

Intent. Both statements are publicly available on the Australian Treasury website (Australian Government, The Treasury, 2016).

> **Box 3.1. Government's expectations and regulators' responses in Australia**
>
> The Australian Government's Statement of Expectations (SoE) outlines its expectations about the role and responsibilities of the ACCC, its relationship with the Government, issues of transparency and accountability and operational matters. It forms part of the Government's commitment to good corporate governance of agencies and reducing the regulatory burden on business and the community. The SoE states that it is imperative that the ACCC act independently and objectively in performing its functions and exercising its powers as set out in the CCA and that the Government expects that the ACCC will take into account the Government's broad policy framework, in performing its role and meeting its responsibilities. The ACCC in turn provides a Statement of Intent (SoI) outlining how it proposes to meet these expectations.
>
> The Australian Energy Regulator has a similar SoE with the Council of Australian Governments Energy Council (COAG EC) in which COAG EC outlines its expectations that the Australian Energy Regulator will perform its legislative functions and implement a work program that supports the objectives set out in the national energy legislation. The SoI sets out the Australian Energy Regulator s work program in regulating energy networks and markets, and the benchmarks that will measure the Australian Energy Regulator s performance. The Statement also sets out how it aims to achieve principles of accountability and transparency, efficient regulation and effective engagement with stakeholders and other energy markets.
>
> *Source:* OECD (2015a), Survey on the independence of economic regulators.

Statements from the executive do not strictly have to be top-down. In fact, it could be a consultative process as is the case for at least two regulators - the Water Industry Commission for Scotland and Nkom. The Scottish regulator publishes its price setting methodology before a draft policy statement on objectives and charging principles is issued for consultation. The statement on charging principles and objectives is finalised following engagement with industry stakeholders and after a draft determination is published by the regulator. In Norway, Nkom proposes goals and priorities to the Ministry of Transport and Communications before it is issued with a statement of expectations.

Also in those cases where statements of expectations are issued, grey areas will inevitably remain as it might be challenging to set clear roles and boundaries between the responsibilities of the executive and those of the regulator. In some cases, the legislative process and Parliament have proven useful in solving deadlocks created by lack of clarity on the boundaries between regulators and governments.

Indicating preferences

Most regulators indicate that governments can participate in public consultations, and when they do so, their submissions are given the same weight as other stakeholders. In some cases, while participation in consultations on draft regulatory decisions is open to all, including the government, the government has not done so in practice. In other cases, government participation in public consultation is compulsory, such as for the Spanish multi-sector regulator, the National Authority for Markets and Competition (*Comisión Nacional de los Mercados y la Competencia*, CNMC) when dealing with the regulation of the telecommunication market. In Canada's case, in order for a federal government department to participate in the National Energy Board (NEB)'s project hearings, it must make the case that it is directly affected by the project, or has relevant information or expertise. This standing test applies to all participants in the NEB's hearings. A number of regulators such as the French Regulatory Authority for Electronic Communications and Postal Services (*Autorité de régulation des communications électroniques et des postes,* ARCEP), the Italian Transport Regulatory Authority (*Autorità di Regolazione dei Trasporti,* ART) and the ESCOSA indicated that although the government is able to participate in public consultations, this almost never happens in practice.

Conversely, public consultation is not a common practice for a few regulators. For example, the Swiss Federal Electricity Commission (ElCom) takes decisions on a case-by-case basis and only in very exceptional circumstances would it proceed through stakeholder submissions.

In addition to public consultation, governments can also use various means to communicate with the regulator, ranging from indirect (media statements) to direct (informal contact and official written correspondence) (Figure 3.3).

Figure 3.3. **How does the government indicate its preferred position regarding regulatory decisions, if it does so?**

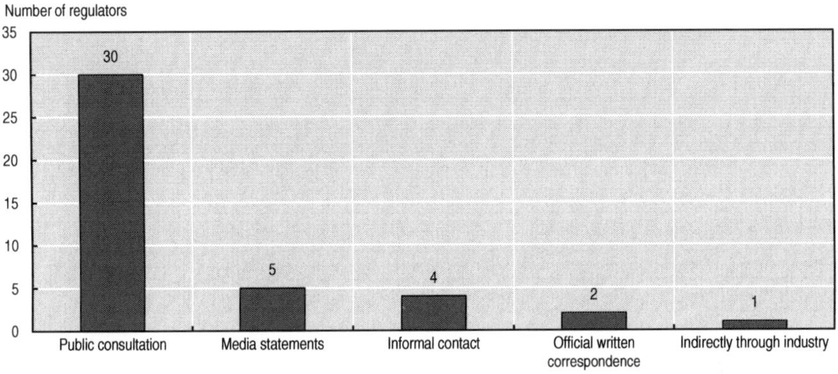

Category	Number of regulators
Public consultation	30
Media statements	5
Informal contact	4
Official written correspondence	2
Indirectly through industry	1

Source: OECD (2015a), OECD Survey on the independence of economic regulators.

The case of the German multi-sector regulator, the Federal Network Agency for Electricity, Gas, Telecommunications, Post and Railway (*Bundesnetzagentur*, BNetzA) is rather unique in that it has a permanent consultative body with parliament rather than the executive: the *Bundesnetzagentur*'s advisory body is composed of representatives of the legislature and has to be consulted for certain regulatory decisions (Box 3.2).

Box 3.2. **The involvement of parliament in a regulator's decisions in Germany**

The Advisory Council of the BNetzA, the German multi-sector regulator, consists of 16 members from all parties represented in the lower house of parliament, the *Bundestag*, and 16 representatives from all parties represented in the upper house, the *Bundesrat*. The Advisory Council can give advice to the BNetzA and, in some cases, defined in legislation (e.g. concerning spectrum allocations by auction), the consent of the Advisory Council is required. The sessions of the Advisory Council are not public.

Source: OECD (2015a), OECD Survey on the independence of economic regulators.

Similarly, regulators are able to make recommendations or issue opinions on draft legislation or policy documents prepared by the government. At times, this role is part of the regulator's formal mandate, and even required by law, especially when involving legislation pertaining to sectors under the regulator's mandate. However, not all regulators' inputs to draft bills are made public.

Some governments comment on regulatory decisions via the media (Figure 3.3). This means of interaction beyond the more formal institutional channels could become a means of exercising some "undue" pressure on the regulator. The media, however, can be also used by regulators to clarify roles and counteract these pressures. This was the case in at least one instance highlighted by a regulator, the French CRE, when a minister indicated the (preferred) outcome of a decision which was in fact under the authority of the regulator. The regulator reacted through a public statement clarifying that the minister had no authority on the matter (Box 3.3).

> **Box 3.3. Government-regulator interactions in the media in France**
>
> In a few cases ministries have used the media to make public commitments in matters that were of the exclusive responsibility of the regulator, which has in turn gone public to clarify the respective roles of the regulator and the ministry. For example, in 2011 the Minister of Energy indicated that electricity smart meters were to be deployed at no cost for users, while the modalities of the coverage of costs were to be defined by the CRE in the network tariff. The Chairman of CRE made a public statement, clarifying the fact that the minister had no authority on the matter.
>
> *Source*: OECD (2015a), OECD Survey on the independence of economic regulators.

Using the media could also heighten political and media scrutiny, resulting in a less effective and conducive regulatory environment. This is also why most regulators seek to consult the government in draft, even if it is not mandatory. Informal contacts are mentioned by four regulators (Figure 3.3). These are interactions that could potentially exercise the strongest pressure and influence as they escape any public scrutiny (contrary for example to formal correspondence) and are difficult to monitor.

Overturning or meddling with regulator decisions

All regulators (with one exception) indicated that the executive is unable to overturn individual decisions that they make and any appeals are settled through the judiciary. In the case of Nkom, the ministry can decide on appeals against decisions made by the regulator and can in certain instances overturn decisions by the regulator (Box 3.4).

> **Box 3.4. Appeals on a regulator's decisions and the role of the Ministry in Norway**
>
> In Norway, the Ministry of Transport and Communications decides on appeals against individual decisions made by the communications regulator, Nkom, and can in some cases reverse or rescind the regulator's decisions. Over the last three years, the Ministry of Transport and Communications has on three occasions overturned decisions made by Nkom, following appeals:
>
> - 2013: Decision regarding compulsory purchase.
> - 2014: Decision on margin squeeze test in the mobile market.
> - 2015: Decision regarding R&D activities for the disabled and other end-users with special needs.
>
> *Source*: OECD (2015a), OECD Survey on the independence of economic regulators.

For certain regulators, the government can, in exceptional situations, intervene in regulator decisions. For example, in the case of the ESCOSA, the government can seek to appeal a decision where it is a party to the decision and may intervene in an appeal brought by a regulated business in some circumstances.

There are, however, cases where the regulator shares functions and powers with the executive and, despite a formal commitment of the executive to safeguarding the independence of the regulator, the practical application of this commitment can be interpreted differently by the executive and the regulator, affecting the relationship between the executive and the regulator (Box 3.5).

> **Box 3.5. Shared functions of the regulator with the executive in the United Kingdom**
>
> The 2013 Strategic Policy Statement to Ofwat from the UK Government, and the 2014 Social and Environmental Guidance from the Welsh Government set the objectives and priorities for the economic regulator of the water and wastewater sector in England and Wales, Ofwat – in the context of Ofwat's statutory duties and functions. The UK Government's 2011 Principles for Economic Regulation set out how and why independence of the economic regulators including Ofwat is important and should be protected. The framework for enforcement (enforcement orders, undertakings and financial penalties) under the Water Industry Act 1991 also allows Ofwat to act independently. However, within this, there is a degree of

> **Box 3.5. Shared functions of the regulator with the executive in the United Kingdom** (*cont.*)
>
> uncertainty as to the extent of this independence. In particular, the framework for enforcement gives Ofwat and the Secretary of State the same powers so if the Department of Environment, Food, and Rural Affairs (Defra) considered that the regulator should be taking action but is not doing so, they would be able to exercise their powers.
>
> This has led to cases where differences of opinion between Ofwat and the government have arisen. An example was the decision on whether the option for retailers to exit the market should be included in the Water Bill, which became the Water Act 2014. Ofwat had argued strongly for approaches which it believed were important in order to perform its duties, including the protection of customers, which was contrary to Defra's position and this had an impact on the regulator's relationship with the executive. Circumstances also occur when the regulator and government agree on the need for independence, but not on what protecting independence means in practice.
>
> *Source:* OECD (2015a), OECD Survey on the independence of economic regulators.

Exchanging and interacting with the regulator (and vice-versa)

The work of regulators and sector ministries inevitably bring the two close to each other. Regulators are often the repository of technical knowledge that can be useful to ministries when developing public policies. A number of regulators have almost daily interactions with staff in ministries.

The role of regulators does not stop there, though. Because regulators have this knowledge, they can also be proactive in signalling particularly relevant issues to the executive and, more broadly, the public debate. There is of course a fine line which might not be always easy to define between remaining within the role of an independent institution and entering the field of policy making (which is ultimately the responsibility of the executives and parliaments).

> **Box 3.6. Walking the fine line between providing advice and making policy in the United Kingdom**
>
> In the United Kingdom, Ofgem, the energy regulator, initiated some work to examine where the market left to its own devices would deliver enough electricity to meet consumers' needs. Under a number of different scenarios, it found a potential problem with security of supply. Ofgem then released a report and subsequently had difficult discussions with ministers and officials who felt that the regulator had gone too far in engaging in "policy".
>
> *Source*: OECD (2015a), OECD Survey on the independence of economic regulators.

Relationship with industry

Regulators' decisions have direct impacts on industry operations. As a result, regulators and industry interact on a daily basis, to exchange information, consult when taking regulatory decisions, ensure compliance and respond to complaints. Regulators will also be inevitably confronted with pressures from industry. These interactions can be formal, through consultations, hearings and public inquiries for the development of regulatory decisions as well as conflictual where the industry can challenge the regulator's decisions through judicial review. Informally, regulators and industry can communicate through the media, public events such as conferences and seminars and informal meetings (Figure 3.4).

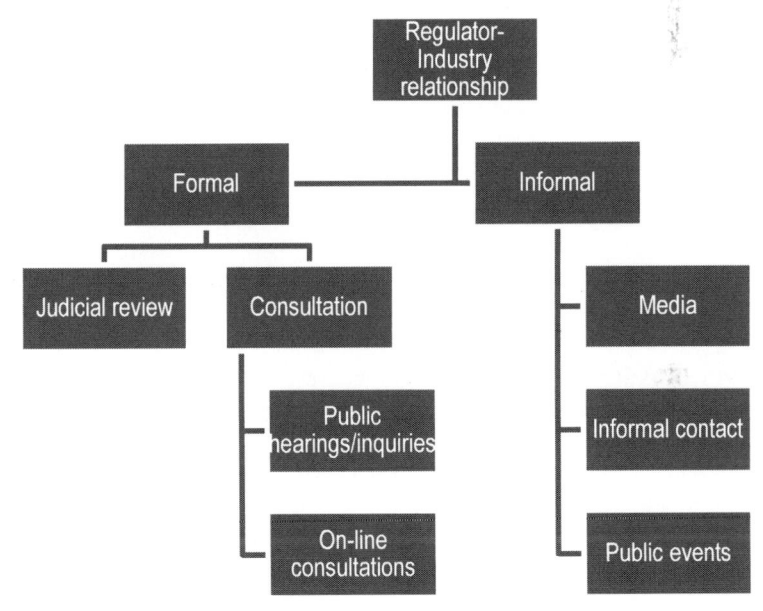

Figure 3.4. **Typology of interactions between industry and regulators**

```
                    Regulator-
                    Industry
                    relationship
                  /              \
              Formal           Informal
             /      \           /    |    \
    Judicial    Consultation  Media  Informal  Public
    review        |                  contact   events
                  Public
                  hearings/inquiries
                  |
                  On-line
                  consultations
```

Source: Based on OECD (2015a), OECD Survey on the independence of economic regulators.

Consulting stakeholders

Public consultations with all stakeholders are the most common formal means of interacting with industry during the development of regulatory decisions. All regulators rely on some formal process for collecting inputs. These processes can include the issuance of consultation papers to be followed by on-line consultations and/or public hearings. A number of regulators make public the results of public consultation on their websites.

In the case of Latvia's multi-sector regulator, the Public Utilities Commission (PUC), stakeholders can request to participate in board meetings, which are open to the public and the minutes of which can be obtained by the public upon request (Box 3.7).

> **Box 3.7. Public consultation in Latvia**
>
> The PUC has established an expanded stakeholder engagement process. Regular public hearings are conducted by the PUC, on top of online consultations, whenever it has to make a decision on tariff setting. Furthermore, utilities are also invited to participate in Board meetings, when there is a topic on agenda concerning a particular service provider. The PUC's Board meetings are open except in cases where confidential issues are considered and everyone has an opportunity to participate in a Board meeting. The time and agenda of a Board meeting are published on the PUC's homepage at least three working days before the meeting so that everybody can find out what issues will be considered and ask to participate.
>
> *Source*: OECD (2015a), OECD Survey on the independence of economic regulators.

Five regulators, including France's ARCEP, the Italian Regulatory Authority for Electricity, Gas and Water (*Autorità per l'energia elettrica, il gas ed il Sistema idrico*, AEEGSI), Mexico's Energy Regulatory Commission (*Comisión Reguladora de Energía*, CRE) and the UK Payment Systems Regulator (PSR), have permanent bodies to facilitate regular exchanges with industry. ARCEP created the *Groupe d'échange entre l'ARCEP, les collectivités territoriales et les opérateurs* (GRACO), which includes representatives of local government in addition to operators. These bodies and groups serve as a platform for public consultation during the development of decisions. They can also serve as a source of information and data on the evolution of the sector overseen by the regulator (Box 3.8).

> **Box 3.8. Regular dialogue with operators and consumers in Italy**
>
> Since 2015, the AEEGSI has a Permanent Observatory of Energy, Water and District Heating Regulation to facilitate a continuous dialogue with representatives of national associations of market operators and consumers and to report on AEEGSI activities, within a broader developing process aimed at enhancing AEEGSI accountability.
>
> The Observatory's functions are mainly to:
>
> - increase stakeholders engagements within decision making processes, with particular regard to market and infrastructure regulation and to consumer protection;

> Box 3.8. **Regular dialogue with operators
> and consumers in Italy** (*cont.*)
>
> - facilitate the acquisition of data and information that may contribute to the preparation of the analysis of the impact of regulation (AIR), as well as for the *ex post* evaluation of policies and implemented decisions of the regulator;
>
> - promote the preparation of consultation documents on matters within the responsibilities of the regulator;
>
> - acquire from representatives of consumer groups, users and end customers, suggestions for evaluating the actual results of the implementation of commitments of regulated entities.
>
> *Source*: OECD (2015a), OECD Survey on the independence of economic regulators; AEEGSI (2015), "Osservatorio permanente della regolazione energetica, idrica e del teleriscaldamento", www.autorita.energia.it/it/osservatorio/home_osservatorio.htm (accessed 15 April 2016).

Some regulators highlighted the risk of capture of public consultation processes by powerful groups, which often have resources and capacity to weigh more heavily. While it is inevitable that those with greater stakes in the decisions of the regulators will try to influence it, regulators appear to be conscious of the risk of "hijacking". Some regulators have been proactive in trying to involve more stakeholders in the process by reaching out to less powerful users and consumers. Regulators have also intensified their communication activities to explain the issues at stake on a particular decision. This can be done through holding general informational events. Norway's Nkom holds several public events on an ad-hoc basis in the form of industry meetings open to all interested parties such as the Nkom Agenda, Frequency Forum, National Group on Numbering, and the Net Neutrality Forum.

Resisting pressures from stakeholders

Beyond formal consultations, stakeholders can try to influence regulators' decisions through lobbying and media campaigns targeting directly the regulator and, more indirectly, through lobbying, media campaigns or informal contacts with ministers and members of parliament (Figure 3.5). Media campaigns can be particularly virulent, sometimes attacking not only the merits of a specific decision but also the legitimacy of the regulator. In those cases where there is a pluralistic media environment, regulators appear to have been able to counteract these media campaigns by using the media themselves to explain their positions and the reasons for the decisions taken by them. Regulators also rely on government-wide lobbying rules (like obligations to register lobbyists and meetings with lobbyists) to make relationship with industry more transparent.

Figure 3.5. **Direct and indirect stakeholder pressures**

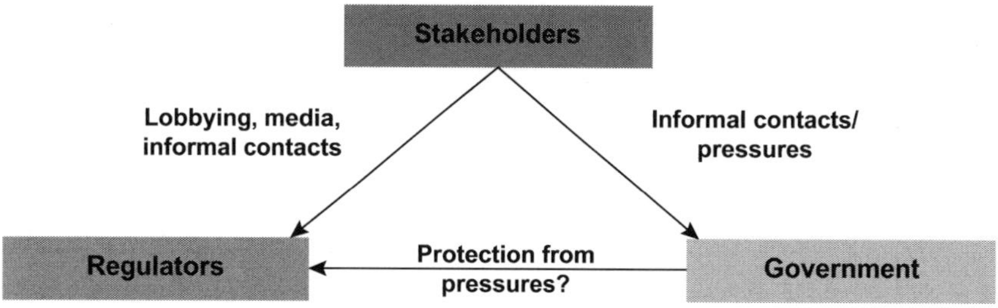

```
                        Stakeholders
                       /            \
     Lobbying, media,/                \Informal contacts/
     informal contacts                 pressures
                   /                    \
                  ↓                      ↓
            Regulators ← Protection from    Government
                         pressures?
```

Source: Based on OECD (2015a), OECD Survey on the independence of economic regulators.

More problematic are those cases where stakeholders (especially industry) can exercise pressures on ministers and members of parliament to affect the decisions of the regulator (Figure 3.5). The effectiveness of these pressures can depend to a large extent on the degree to which the regulator is protected from (undue) pressures from the executive and parliament. However, elected governments are ultimately responsible for determining the mandate and powers of regulators and these interventions can impact the power and role of the regulator. Some regulators have in part counteracted this risk by going public on these issues and stirring at least a public debate among the citizens to whom governments are accountable.

To avoid being subject to industry pressure and potential conflicts of interest, some regulators have instituted strong transparency/disclosure requirements for their staff and activities. The Canadian NEB commits to the *NEB Code of Conduct* which aligns with the Canadian *Values and Ethics Code for the Public Sector*. Article 2.1.6 of the NEB Code sets out expectations that an employee's work and interests must be divested from real, potential or apparent conflicts of interest. This includes disclosure of relevant employee assets and interests, keeping the NEB informed about any potential conflict of interest scenarios and defining parameters for where gifts, hospitality and benefits offered by industry are unacceptable.

Communicating with stakeholders

Regulators are conscious of the risk of undue pressures from and conflict with stakeholders on their activities and ultimately their independence. While judicial review is the legitimate way of solving conflicts with stakeholders, this can be costly. Accordingly, regulators have been particularly active in communicating on their role and functions (in addition to regulatory decisions), in order to create trust and confidence among industry and consumers. Some regulators regularly use new electronic media like Twitter and Facebook to communicate. Other regulators have been active in reaching out to stakeholders on strategic directions for the regulated sector, facilitating contributions from industry and consumers. A salient example of strengthening interactions with stakeholders through informal means such as the media is provided by the Spanish CNMC (Box 3.9).

Box 3.9. Developing a communication policy through the media in Spain

As part of its efforts to bolster communication, the CNMC is making extensive use of media channels to explain its objectives and the reasoning behind its decision. In 2014, the CNMC:

- Issued 216 press releases.
- Held 5 press conferences.
- Organised 98 meetings with media.

Other communication tools, such as the CNMC blog or the transparency portal, are also frequently used.

Source: OECD (2015a), OECD Survey on the independence of economic regulators.

Merely conducting public consultations is often not sufficient and regulators should also seek to address the comments and explain their rationale when accepting or rejecting them. This is for example the approach developed by the Peruvian regulators, Osiptel and Osinergmin (Box 3.10).

Box 3.10. Transparent treatment of inputs during public consultation in Peru

Osiptel, the Peruvian communications regulator, and Osinergmin, the Peruvian energy and mines regulator, publish all comments received in a document called "Matrix of Comments (*Matriz de comentarios*)", where the regulators explains why some comments were accepted and others were dismissed. This matrix is published along with the final resolution. Some examples include:

- Setting of the Mobile termination rates for the 2015-18 period, https://www.osiptel.gob.pe/articulo/031-2015-cd-osiptel

> **Box 3.10. Transparent treatment of inputs during public consultation in Peru** (*cont.*)
>
> - Amendment of Consumer Protection Code on Telecommunications Services, https://www.osiptel.gob.pe/articulo/056-2015-cd-osiptel
> - Regulation on the Handling of Users' Complaints, https://www.osiptel.gob.pe/articulo/047-2015-cd-osiptel
> - General rule for regulatory accounting, www.osinergmin.gob.pe/seccion/centro_documental/PlantillaMarcoLegal Busqueda/RCD%20003-2016-OS.CD.pdf
>
> *Source:* OECD (2015a), OECD Survey on the independence of economic regulators.

The frequency of communication with stakeholders also plays a big part in ensuring good relations. In addition to making sure all pertinent information is publicly available on the website, the Alberta Energy Regulator also publishes a Regulatory Change Report on a weekly basis highlighting progress on the different stages through which a regulatory decision is going (e.g. planned, in progress, completed or suspended).

Getting a broad spectrum of representation at public consultation and hearings is essential to ensure effective and inclusive public participation and consideration of public concerns prior to regulatory decisions. For example, the NEB offers participant funding to non-industry not-for-profit groups and individuals to prepare information on the potential impacts of a project and participate in public hearings.

Perceptions of independence

The media sometimes convey contradictory views on the independence of regulators. In one case, the same regulator was described as being too close to industry and too close to government. This can depend on the specific issue at stake but also the different biases of the media. Some regulators have conducted public opinion surveys which typically focus on the level of public awareness of regulator activities but some also incorporate questions on the value and perception of the work that regulators do. Latvia's PUC, for example, has commissioned an annual public perception survey to both users and regulated industries since 2013.

Staff

The people who work in a regulatory agency play an essential role in shaping the culture of independence that permeates the work of a regulator. Such a culture can be contingent on the way in which the board/head, management and professionals are recruited, conduct their work and exit the agency. Undue influence can undermine this culture of independence and be exercised at different junctures and entry points. Figure 3.6 maps some of the critical points where staff can be confronted with "undue" pressure and influence.

Figure 3.6. **Protecting staff from undue influence**

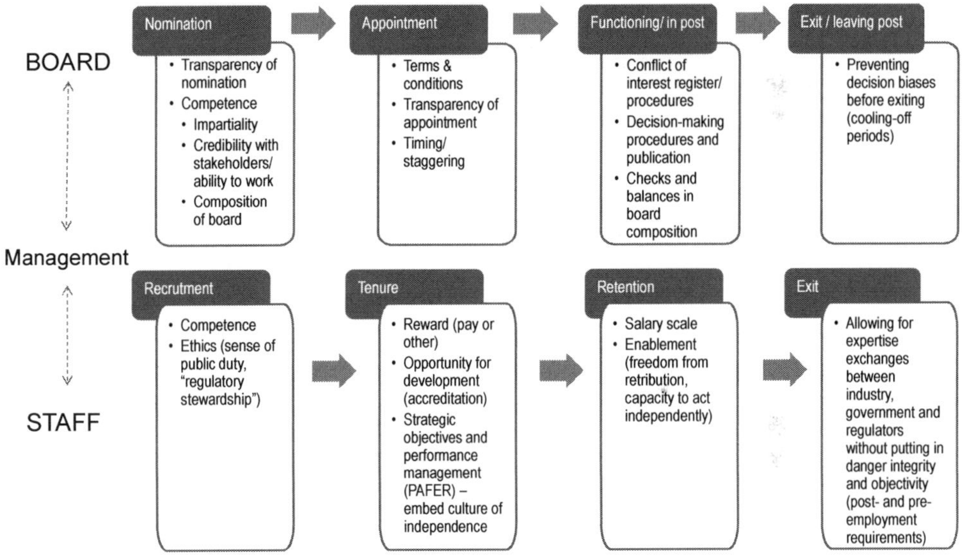

BOARD

Nomination
- Transparency of nomination
- Competence
- Impartiality
- Credibility with stakeholders/ ability to work
- Composition of board

Appointment
- Terms & conditions
- Transparency of appointment
- Timing/ staggering

Functioning/ in post
- Conflict of interest register/ procedures
- Decision-making procedures and publication
- Checks and balances in board composition

Exit / leaving post
- Preventing decision biases before exiting (cooling-off periods)

Management

STAFF

Recruitment
- Competence
- Ethics (sense of public duty, "regulatory stewardship")

Tenure
- Reward (pay or other)
- Opportunity for development (accreditation)
- Strategic objectives and performance management (PAFER) – embed culture of independence

Retention
- Salary scale
- Enablement (freedom from retribution, capacity to act independently)

Exit
- Allowing for expertise exchanges between industry, government and regulators without putting in danger integrity and objectivity (post- and pre-employment requirements)

Source: Based on OECD (2015a), OECD Survey on the independence of economic regulators.

Professional staff

Professional staff can be less exposed to pressures from either politicians or industry lobbyists as their role in regulatory decisions is less prominent. While direct pressure can be less strong, professional staff is nevertheless expected to provide the technical and objective advice that help the board/agency head take unbiased decisions. In this respect, a culture of independence can help foster an environment that helps staff produce that needed unbiased advice. This culture can start with transparent and unbiased selection and appointment processes; it is reinforced by clear accountability lines and responsibilities for the professional body of the agency (*vis-à-vis* the board, for example) and the development of an organisational culture that fosters public service values. Challenging and interesting work in an environment that puts importance into non-monetary "soft" incentives like attention to work-life balance and the possibility to grow rapidly within the organisation can help compensate for possible gaps between the remuneration of regulators and salaries and bonuses that are paid by the regulated industry (Figure 3.6).

Recruitment

Virtually all regulators are relatively free to set their own recruitment criteria and run their own recruitment through public advertisements of available positions and the establishment of selection panels. Some regulators use recruitment agencies and often include independent members in recruitment panels. Final appointments of professional staff and management staff are usually made by the professional body of the regulators, either through the chief executive officer/director general/secretary general or the selection panel established for that purpose. For 9 regulators, including AEEGSI, ART, PUC, Portugal's Water and Waste Services Regulation Authority (*Entidade Reguladora dos Serviços de Aguas e Residuos*, ERSAR), Turkey's Energy Market Regulatory Authority (EMRA) and ElCom, the board is responsible for the final appointment of professional staff (and for four regulators, the board appoints staff together with the head of the professional body). For example, in the case of the Italian public utilities regulators (AEEGSI, AGCOM and ART), the recruitment of professional and management staff follows the evaluation and assessment of candidates by an independent selection panel and as result of an open competition. The Board adopts a final decision approving the procedures carried out by the selection panel. The recruitment is ultimately carried out by the Head of human resources (Figure 3.7).

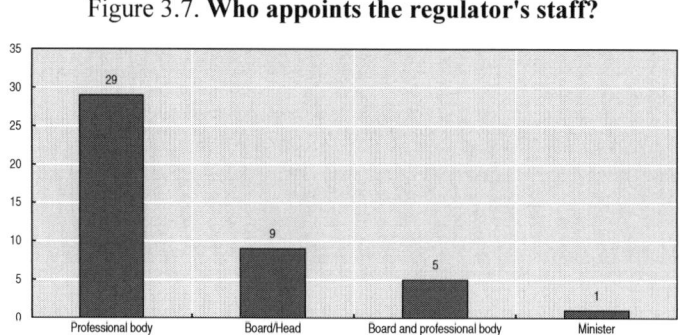

Figure 3.7. **Who appoints the regulator's staff?**

Professional body	Board/Head	Board and professional body	Minister
29	9	5	1

Note: No information for 4 regulators.

Source: OECD (2015a), OECD Survey on the independence of economic regulators.

In a number of cases, regulators follow public service general rules in the recruitment process, but ministries never interfere with recruitment. Public service rules do not seem to undermine the independence of the regulator. On the contrary, they appear to add transparency, guarantee fairness in the recruitment process and help mark a clear difference between the regulator and the regulated industry.

Tenure/term in office

Reporting/accountability

Professional staff reports to senior management who can either report to the Board and/or the chair of the board or to a head of the professional body (for example, a chief executive officer, director general or secretary general) who in turn reports to the board and/or the chair (Figure 3.8).

Senior management, which are often on open-ended/civil service contracts, can help mark a distinction between the board, inevitably more exposed to external pressures, and the professional body of the regulator, helping shield the professional staff from some of those pressures. In those cases where the head of the professional staff has an office term that is longer than that of the board, the head of the professional staff can also guarantee some continuity in the management of the agency (beyond the terms of the board) (Figure 3.8).

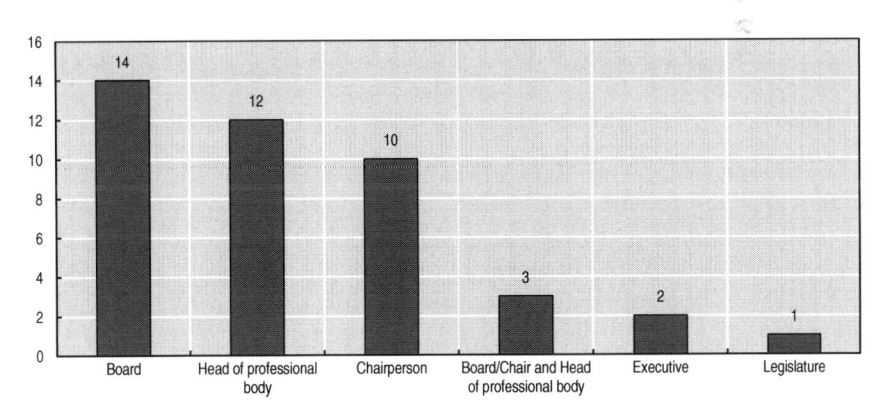

Figure 3.8. **To whom is senior management responsible to?**

Category	Count
Board	14
Head of professional body	12
Chairperson	10
Board/Chair and Head of professional body	3
Executive	2
Legislature	1

Note: No information for 7 regulators.

Source: OECD (2015a), OECD Survey on the independence of economic regulators.

Ethic codes and training

Creating a distinctive organisational culture with a strong focus on the independence of the organisation can help create an environment that is less prone to pressure from government and industry. Twenty-six regulators have codes of ethics to foster values of independence and objectivity among professional staff (and the Board). Sixteen of them have developed their own codes of ethics, 9 rely on the public service code of ethics and four have added a regulator-specific code to the public service code (Figure 3.9). In two regulatory agencies, the implementation of the code of ethics is overseen by an ombudsman external to the organisation.

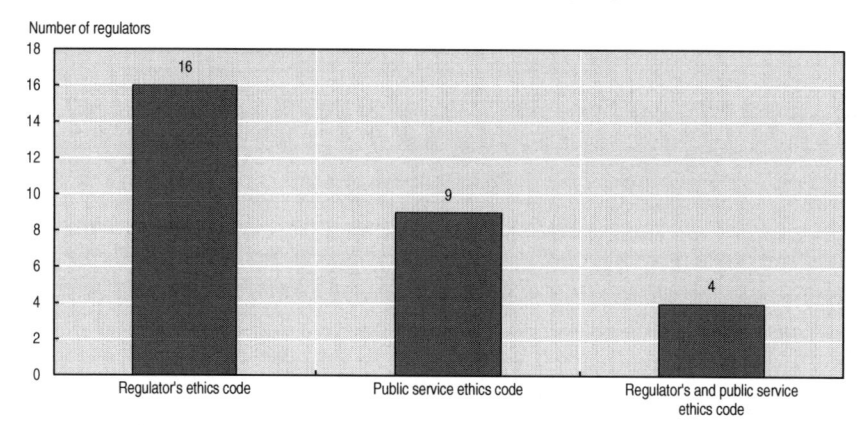

Figure 3.9. **Use of ethics codes among regulators**

Category	Number of regulators
Regulator's ethics code	16
Public service ethics code	9
Regulator's and public service ethics code	4

Source: OECD (2015a), OECD Survey on the independence of economic regulators.

Retention

The majority of regulators – 27 – follow the government remuneration policy. Fourteen regulators have their own salary policy, which can be (and has been) nevertheless affected by wider public sector policies like spending reviews. In some cases, the regulator can set its own salary scale within a total remuneration budget set by the government. Seven regulators follow the government remuneration policy with some leeway for example in setting bonuses and topping up the basic civil service salary (Figure 3.10).

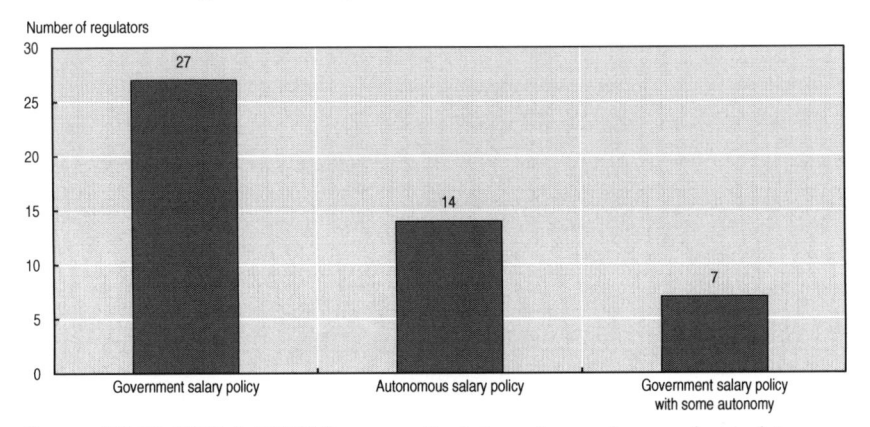

Figure 3.10. **Regulators' remuneration policies**

Policy	Number of regulators
Government salary policy	27
Autonomous salary policy	14
Government salary policy with some autonomy	7

Source: OECD (2015a), OECD Survey on the independence of economic regulators.

Regardless of who sets the remuneration policy, the key issue is ultimately whether the regulator is capable of attracting and, equally important, retaining staff. Professionals working in regulatory agencies share a number of skills and competencies with the regulated industry, which is more competitive in terms of salaries and bonuses. Inevitably, regulators will lose some staff to the regulated industry, especially at the senior level and might find it difficult to attract some highly specialised staff. However, more than 60% of regulators did not signal particular problems in attracting and retaining their professional staff. While the majority of those who do face problems are bound to public service salary scales, three (out of 14) have salary policies that are independent from the overall civil service remuneration policy (Figure 3.11), including Portugal's ERSAR and the Alberta Energy Regulator. In these cases, however, the government could still have a large say over regulators' salary policies (Box 3.11).

Box 3.11. Remuneration policy independent of civil service salary policy in Portugal

ERSAR is entitled by law to have a different remuneration policy from other civil servants. The salary of the members of the Board is established by a remuneration commission which is composed of three members: one appointed by the Ministry of Finance, one appointed by the Ministry responsible for the economic activity which ERSAR regulates and one appointed by ERSAR. The determination of the remunerations is made according to the complexity of the sector, the remuneration benchmark within the regulated industry and other relevant criteria.

Source: OECD (2015a), OECD Survey on the independence of economic regulators.

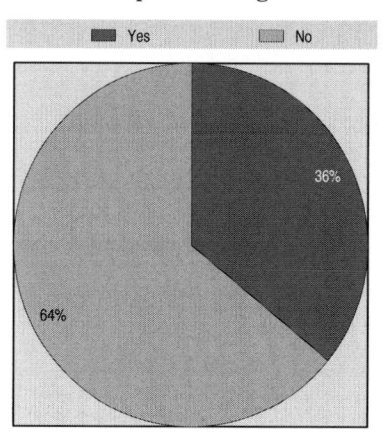

Figure 3.11. **Is it an issue finding competent and skilled staff for an independent organisation?**

[Pie chart: Yes 36%, No 64%]

Note: Data based on 39 answers; 9 regulators did not answer the question.

Source: OECD (2015a), OECD Survey on the independence of economic regulators.

Regulators have been able to develop human resources policies that can help compensate for the remuneration gap with the private sector. These policies can include a particular attention for work-life balance. A number of regulators pointed to the sense of serving a public purpose, the interest and challenge of the tasks staff accomplish and a strong culture of independence as important factors in attracting and retaining capable staff.

Exit

Most regulators have some restrictions for professional staff leaving the agency to work in the regulated industry. Twelve regulators have cooling-off periods of 1 to 3 years (mostly for senior management). In the case of the Italian public utilities regulators (AEEGSI, AGCOM and ART), a law adopted in 2014 introduced a 2-year cooling-off period for the management that is neither remunerated nor compensated. Some regulators, like the Canadian NEB, apply cooling-off periods across all staff (Box 3.12). For six regulators, professional staff is subject to the civil service-wide rules imposing some requirements for notifying potential conflict of interests either to the regulator or a deontology body after leaving their job. In two regulatory agencies –PSR and Ofgem in the United Kingdom – professional staff work on "non-sensitive issues" or are put on leave for a certain period of time before they take up a position in the regulated industry. Eighteen regulators do not have any restriction (Figure 3.12).

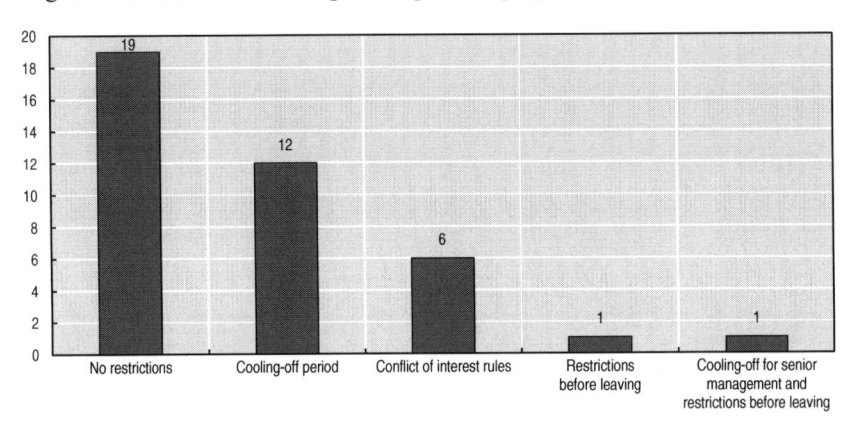

Figure 3.12. **Restrictions on pre- or post-employment of professional staff**

Category	Count
No restrictions	19
Cooling-off period	12
Conflict of interest rules	6
Restrictions before leaving	1
Cooling-off for senior management and restrictions before leaving	1

Note: No answer for 9 regulators.

Source: OECD (2015a), OECD Survey on the independence of economic regulators.

Box 3.12. Applying cooling-off period to all professional staff at Canada's NEB

The NEB has post-employment restrictions of one year for former employees. For the first year after leaving the NEB, an employee must not represent a company or individual before the NEB. This includes: sitting as a witness; acting as counsel; serving as an official representative at hearings; signing correspondence sent to the Board; or attending meetings with the Board or NEB employees. During this time; however, it is acceptable for a former employee to make routine requests for information. Once employees leave the NEB they must still continue to keep confidential NEB information that is not publicly available.

Source: OECD (2015a), OECD Survey on the independence of economic regulators.

Board

The board or the agency head (for the three regulators who do not have a board) ultimately take the decisions for which the regulator will be held accountable and can be exposed to greater pressures than professional staff. As the government (executive and/or parliament) is responsible for the nomination and appointment of the board members and the agency head, board members and heads can be closer (or at least have more intense relations with) the nominating and appointing authority at least before they start their "tour of duty". The nomination is a critical juncture where perceptions of undue proximity could be strong. Means like independent search committees are sometimes used to ensure that the nomination process is based on competence and dispel any sense of proximity or dependence that could impair the capacity of the regulator to *act independently* in its decisions.

During their tour of duty, board members and heads inevitably interact with governments and parliaments, as well as industry. The impact of these interactions on the decisions can in part depend on the transparency of the relationship between the board/head and the appointing authority, the administrative culture in which the regulator and the government operates and the sense of professionalism and objectivity that the regulator as an institution has developed. Safeguards like fixed terms, clear rules for dismissing board members as well as conflict of interest and cooling-off periods can minimise the opportunities for undue pressures and help dispel perceptions of cosiness with industry (Figure 3.13).

Nomination

For most regulators, the executive nominates the board members. The nomination can be made either by the cabinet or the prime minister upon proposal of the relevant sector minister or directly by the sector minister. A few regulators reported that the nomination by the executive usually happen "behind closed doors", with little transparency and information on why and how a nominee is chosen.

For five regulators, the nomination is made by selection committees usually composed of sector ministries, the regulator and some external experts. This is the case, for example, for the UK PSR, Peru's Osiptel and Osinergmin and Mexico's Federal Institute of Telecommunications (*Instituto Federal de Telecomunicaciones*, IFT). For three regulators, the nomination is made by an external selection panel. For example, in the case of the Australian Energy Regulator, there is an independent panel that interviews potential nominees for Board appointments, before making a recommendation to the Minister who also seek the agreement of the States and Territories. Selection panels and committees usually issue public calls for nominations in the media to solicit applications and conduct interviews before identifying potential nominees.

For the French energy and electronic communications regulators (CRE and ARCEP), the presidents of the higher and lower parliamentary chambers nominate (and appoint) some board members. In the case of the German BNetzA, the nominee is proposed by a special advisory body composed of members of the higher and lower parliamentary chambers (Figure 3.13).

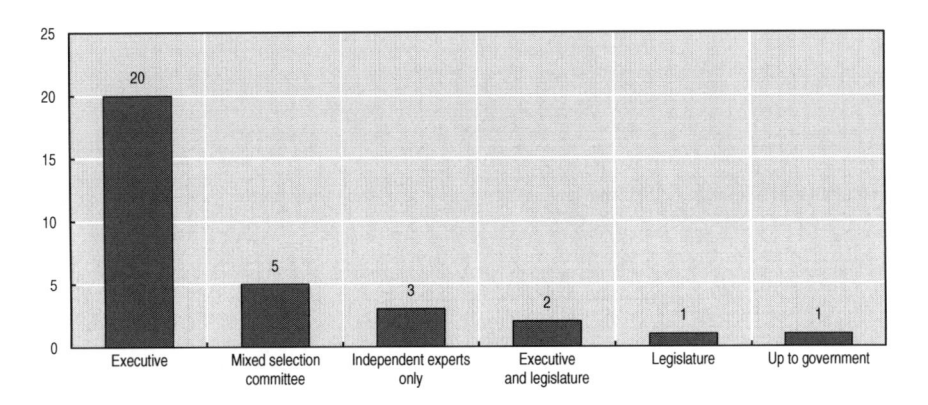

Figure 3.13. Authority nominating the board/head

Authority	Count
Executive	20
Mixed selection committee	5
Independent experts only	3
Executive and legislature	2
Legislature	1
Up to government	1

Notes: No information on the nominating authority for 13 regulators; for two regulators the nomination of some board members is made by the executive and some by the legislature.

Source: OECD (2015a), OECD Survey on the independence of economic regulators.

For the Alberta Energy Regulator, the nomination process of its board is decided at the discretion of the government, which can choose to publicly advertise positions, use a recruitment agency or use an independent selection panel. The authority of the board is specified in the Responsible Energy Development Act, the Alberta Energy Regulator's enabling legislation.

Appointment

For most regulators, the executive is ultimately responsible for appointing the board/head. In the cases where the head of state formally appoints the board/head, the nomination usually comes from the executive, leaving the appointment *de facto* in the hands of the executive (cabinet, prime minister or sector minister). For 7 regulators, the appointment is made by parliament. In one case – the UK PSR – the board is appointed by another regulator, the Financial Conduct Authority (Figure 3.14).

The appointment process appears more transparent than the nomination. For at least eight regulators, the nominee of the executive has to undergo parliamentary hearings and a formal vote of parliamentary committees.

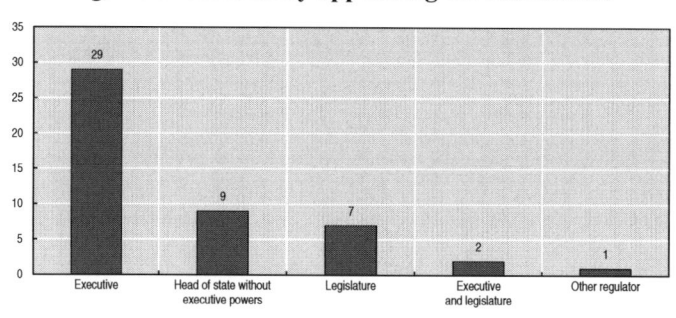

Figure 3.14. **Authority appointing the board/head**

Authority	Count
Executive	29
Head of state without executive powers	9
Legislature	7
Executive and legislature	2
Other regulator	1

Source: OECD (2015a), OECD Survey on the independence of economic regulators.

For the French energy and electronic communications regulators (CRE and ARCEP respectively), the nomination and appointment of some board members is made by the executive (the legislature being involved through a hearing and an opinion), and some by the legislature, in practice the presidents of both chambers of parliament appoint one or two board members each. There is a conscious effort to have gender balance in the composition of the board (Box 3.13).

> Box 3.13. **Appointment and nomination of board members by the executive and the legislature in France**
>
> The French energy code provides that CRE's Board of Commissioners comprises six members, while respecting parity between men and women. The President of the Board is appointed by a decree of the President of the Republic upon proposal of the Prime Minister, following public hearings and a formal opinion on the nominee expressed by the relevant parliamentary committees. Three members of the Board are also appointed by a decree of the President of the Republic, one of them upon proposal of the Minister in charge of the French Overseas Territories based on the person's knowledge and experience of non-interconnected areas. The Presidents of the National Assembly and the Senate appoints two additional members of the Board each (one based on the person's knowledge and qualifications in the field of data protection and the other in the field of local energy services).
>
> Similarly, the French postal and electronic communications code sets the requirements for the nomination and appointment of the seven board members of the ARCEP. Similarly to the CRE, the President of the Board is appointed by a decree of the President of the Republic upon proposal of the Prime Minister, following public hearings and a formal opinion on the nominee expressed by the relevant parliamentary committees. The President of the Republic also appoints two members of the Board. The Presidents of the National Assembly and the Senate appoints two Board members each.
>
> *Source*: OECD (2015a), OECD Survey on the independence of economic regulators.

Tour of duty

For 41 regulators, board members have a fixed term with clear rules for the removal of the board member. With the exception of Nkom whose head has no set term, terms of regulator boards are typically longer than the term of the appointing authority (Figure 3.15). The term of Nkom's head ends either when he/she resigns or when he/she is removed by the King in Council in case of violating Norwegian laws. Reasons for such removal of the head are not usually made public.

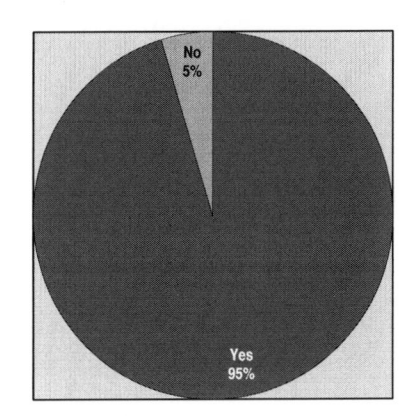

Figure 3.15. **Is there security of tenure for board members/head?**

Note: No information available for 5 regulators.

Source: OECD (2015a), OECD Survey on the independence of economic regulators.

For fifteen regulators, board members have staggered terms that ensure some continuity, institutional memory and stability for the work of the board. Two regulators are considering the introduction of staggered terms. In the case of the Italian public utilities regulators – AEEGSI, AGCOM and ART – the entire board is renewed every 7 years and no Board member can be reappointed for another term.

Exit

Twenty-four regulators have restrictions on the kind of employment that board members and agency heads can take up after leaving the regulatory agency. These "cooling-off" periods usually prevent the board member to work in the regulated industry (but does not prevent him/her to return to his/her public service job) (Figure 3.16).

Figure 3.16. **Are there restrictions on post-employment of board members/head?**

Category	Number
No	13
Yes (cooling-off period)	24
No but conflict of interest rules	2

Note: No information for 9 regulators.

Source: OECD (2015a), OECD Survey on the independence of economic regulators.

Cooling-off periods are mostly limited to 1 year (8 regulators) and 2 years (10 regulators). The French CRE has a cooling-off period of 3 years. The cooling-off period for the Italian public utilities regulators – AEEGSI, AGCOM and ART – was recently reduced from 4 to 2 years (see Figure 3.17). With the exception of the Portuguese water and waste regulator (ERSAR) and the Turkish energy regulator (EMRA), former board members and agency heads do not receive any remuneration during the cooling-off period. In the case of ERSAR, for two years after the end of appointment, members of the Board cannot establish any contract with organisations over which ERSAR exercises its intervention, receiving half of the monthly remuneration as compensation.

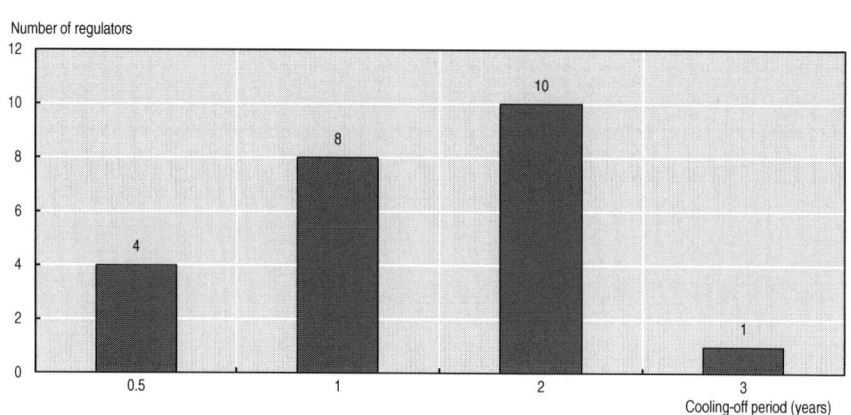

Figure 3.17. **Length of cooling-off period for board members/head**

Number of regulators

Cooling-off period (years)	Number of regulators
0.5	4
1	8
2	10
3	1

Source: OECD (2015a), OECD Survey on the independence of economic regulators.

In some cases, these restrictions have influenced the composition of boards, which tend to include either people with industry experience who are at the end of their career or civil servants who can return to the civil service job after the end of their term.

Budget

Appropriate funding of the regulator is essential to determine the extent to which the regulator can carry out its mandate and *act independently*. The source of the funding could be less relevant than the way in which funding needs are determined, funds are decided and the extent to which the regulator can manage these funds autonomously (Figure 3.18).

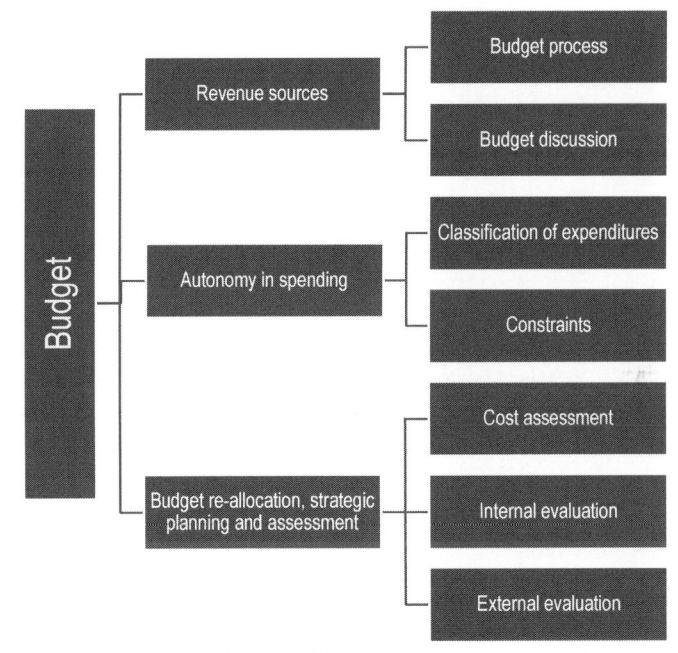

Figure 3.18. **Independence entry point for budgeting**

- Budget
  - Revenue sources
    - Budget process
    - Budget discussion
  - Autonomy in spending
    - Classification of expenditures
    - Constraints
  - Budget re-allocation, strategic planning and assessment
    - Cost assessment
    - Internal evaluation
    - External evaluation

Source: Based on OECD (2015a), OECD Survey on the independence of economic regulators.

Funding sources

Half of the regulators are funded through fees paid by the regulated industry (and to a less extent by licenses and fines). Eleven regulators are financed through general revenues and thirteen regulators through a blend of fees and general revenues (although in these cases the majority of the funding tends to come from fees) (Figure 3.19).

Regardless of the funding source, regulators' funds are mostly appropriated through the national budget. Parliamentary appropriation seems to guarantee transparency and accountability to the process. In the case of the Italian public utilities regulators (AEEGSI, AGCOM and ART), the Peruvian energy and communication regulators (Osinergmin and Osiptel), and the Turkish energy regulator (EMRA), fees are collected directly by the regulator and do not go through the national treasury and a parliamentary appropriation. In some of these cases, the regulator's budget still has to be approved by the cabinet or the sector minister. For example, for the Italian public utilities regulators (AEEGSI, AGCOM and ART), the maximum fee is fixed by law. On a yearly basis each regulator proposes a fee, which is approved by the Ministry of Economy and the Prime Minister Cabinet.

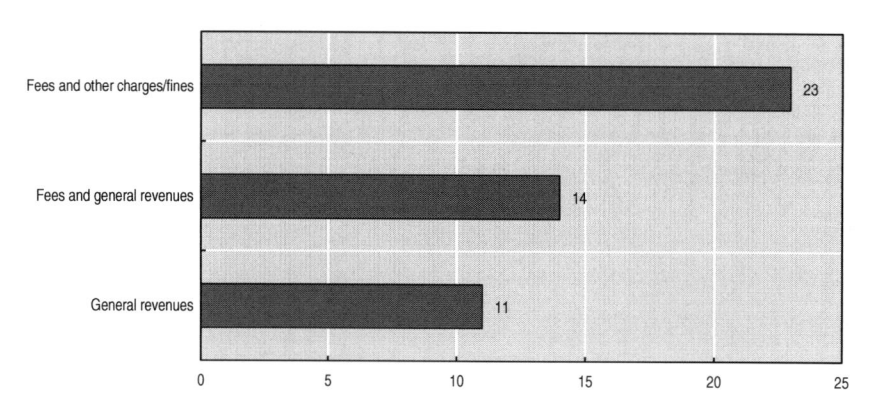

Figure 3.19. **Regulators' funding sources**

Funding source	Count
Fees and other charges/fines	23
Fees and general revenues	14
General revenues	11

Source: OECD (2015a), OECD Survey on the independence of economic regulators.

Determining the fees

Fees to the regulated industry are usually either set as a percentage of the net turnover or income, or based on the activity level of the operators. The latter methodology is used by ERSAR, whose levy on industries has a component depending on the activity level of the operators (cubic meters of water supplied or wastewater drained/treated or tonnes of waste collected/treated). In both cases, larger operators/industry players would generally contribute more to the regulator's funding.

Among the regulators that are funded in part or fully by fees, 19 are responsible for setting the fees or making a fee proposal to the ministry or the cabinet which formally approve the fee. In the case of eight regulators, the government sets the fee without a formal submission of the regulator (Figure 3.20).

Figure 3.20. **Who sets the regulatory fee?**

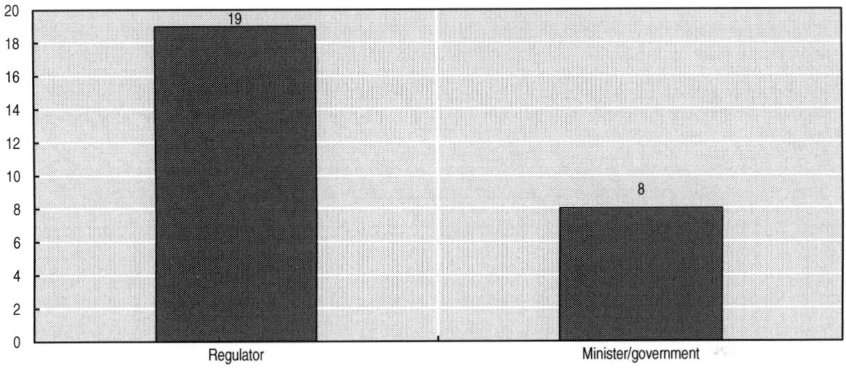

Regulator	Minister/government
19	8

Note: No information for 9 regulators.

Source: OECD (2015a), OECD Survey on the independence of economic regulators.

Where the minister or the cabinet sets the fees, some issues could emerge. For example, in the case of the Latvian multi-sector regulator (PUC), where the cabinet of ministers sets the fees within a legislated ceiling and ministries have controlling stakes in regulated companies, the council of ministers reduced the level of the fee during the global financial crisis from 0.2% to 0.17%.

Other regulators have established a structured and consultative process to estimate the costs of the regulator's activities and therefore the charges for the regulated industry. The Canadian NEB, for example, premises cost recovery on commodity charging; costs are allocated to the principle commodities regulated by the NEB before being allocated to specific entities within those sectors (oil – oil pipelines, gas – gas pipelines, etc.). Companies pay their share of recoverable costs through greenfield levies, fixed levies (small, intermediate companies and other commodities) or proportional levies (large companies). The allocation of costs to commodity categories is based on time spent on each commodity. The NEB also has an advisory committee, which is composed of the staff from the regulator and representatives of the regulated companies, that reviews planned expenditures and discusses cost recovery issues. It can also request supplementary funding from the federal government for special programs, and unexpected or exceptional activities. This is done according to a structured process that boosts accountability (Box 3.14).

> **Box 3.14. Structured process for requesting additional funds in Canada**
>
> Supplementary funding is discussed between the NEB and the Minister of Natural Resources and a recommendation is made to the Minister of Finance, who controls the national budget. The national budget, usually announced in February/March by the Minister of Finance, allocates funds to the NEB under broad purposes for spending obligations. For example, additional temporary funds were received in the 2012-13 fiscal year to enhance NEB safety and security programs as well as public awareness. Temporary funding for five fiscal years beginning in 2015-16 was received for safety and environmental protection and greater engagement with Canadians.
>
> Following the announcement of the supplementary funding, the NEB prepares a submission to the Treasury Board of Canada that outlines specific programs with a detailed plan describing how the funds will be used. The Treasury Board ensures that the funds support whole-of-government priorities and demonstrates "value for money".
>
> *Source*: OECD (2015a), OECD Survey on the independence of economic regulators.

Appropriating general revenues

Among the regulators that are funded in part or fully by general revenues, 11 regulators receive annual appropriations, whereas 2 regulators – Ofgem and the French energy regulator (CRE) – negotiate their appropriations over a 3 to 4 year period (Figure 3.21). Budget appropriations for the French regulator are negotiated on a three-year basis, although some flexibility on certain areas remains on an annual basis. Multi-annual negotiations also concern staff ceilings which have to be respected by the regulator. In the case of Mexico's energy regulators – CRE and the National Hydrocarbons Commission (*Comisión Nacional de Hidrocarburos*, CNH), the budget appropriations are authorised by Congress on an annual basis. Nevertheless, because the energy reform that was introduced by the government widened the responsibilities of both regulators, Congress approved budgetary appropriations for the period 2015-18, in order to guarantee that regulators would have enough resources to implement the reform and perform their new duties. While a multi-annual budget is no guarantee of sufficient resources, an annual budget allocation can offer more frequent opportunities for putting into question or reducing the regulator's budget.

Figure 3.21. **Timeline of budget appropriations**

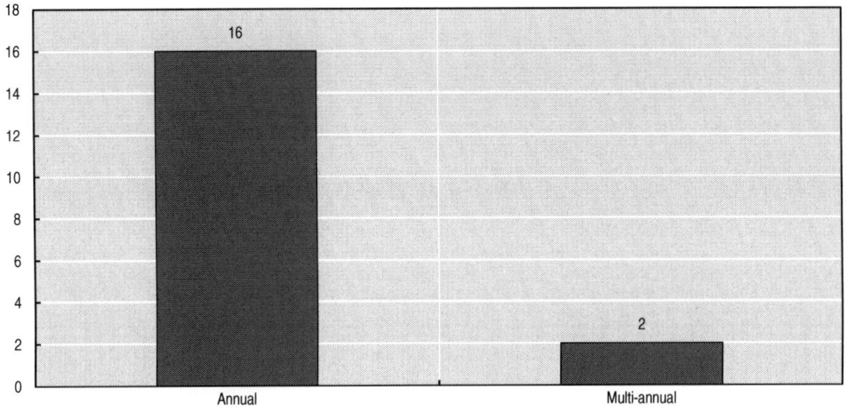

Category	Value
Annual	16
Multi-annual	2

Note: No information for 6 regulators.

Source: OECD (2015a), OECD Survey on the independence of economic regulators.

References

Australian Government, The Treasury (2016), "Statement of Intent", www.treasury.gov.au/policy-topics/publicpolicyandgovt/~/link.aspx?_id=db7094eb11244c9192e44870f7aed7ac&_z=z (accessed 15 April 2016).

AEEGSI (2015), "Osservatorio permanente della regolazione energetica, idrica e del teleriscaldamento", www.autorita.energia.it/it/osservatorio/home_osservatorio.htm (accessed 15 April 2016).

OECD (2015b), *OECD Regulatory Policy Outlook 2015*, OECD Publishing, Paris, http://dx.doi.org/10.1787/9789264238770-en.

OECD (2015a), OECD Survey on the independence of economic regulators.

Annex A

Key bibliographical references

AEEGSI (2015), "Osservatorio permanente della regolazione energetica, idrica e del teleriscaldamento", www.autorita.energia.it/it/osservatorio/home_osservatorio.htm (accessed 15 April 2016).

Alesina, A. et al. (2005), "Regulation and Investment", *Journal of the European Economic Association*, Vol. 3/4, pp. 791- 825.

Andres, L., J.L. Guasch, and S.L. Azumendi (2008), "Regulatory Governance and Sector Performance: Methodology and Evaluation for Electricity Distribution in Latin America", *Policy Research Working Paper*, No. 4494.

Andres, L. et al. (2007), "Assessing the Governance of Electricity Regulatory Agencies in the Latin American and Caribbean Region: A Benchmarking Analysis", *Policy Research Working Paper 4380*, November.

Armstrong, M. and D.E. Sappington (2007), "Recent Developments in the Theory of Regulation", in Armstrong, M. and R. Porter (eds.), *Handbook of Industrial Organization (Vol. III)*, pp. 1557-1700, Elsevier Science Publishers, Amsterdam.

Bach, T. and E. Ruffing (2013), "Networking for Autonomy? National Agencies in European Networks", *Public Administration*, Vol. 91/3, pp. 712-726.

Bauer, J.M. (2003), "The coexistence of regulation, state ownership and competition in infrastructure industries", *Quello Center Working Paper*, No. 03-03, Quello center for telecommunications management and law, Michigan state university, http://papers.ssrn.com/sol3/papers.cfm?abstract_id=397060 (accessed May 2016).

Bawn, K. (1995), "Political Control Versus Expertise: Congressional Choices about Administrative Procedures", *American Political Science Review*, Vol. 89/1, pp. 62-73.

Besley, T. and A. Case (2000), "Unnatural Experiments? Estimating the Incidence of Exogenous Policies", *Economic Journal*, Vol. 110/467, pp. F672-F694.

Bortolotti, B. et al. (2011), "Capital Structure and Regulation: Do Ownership and Regulatory Independence Matter?", *Journal of Economics and Management Strategy*, Vol. 20/2, pp. 517-564.

Cambini, C. and L. Rondi (2014), "Independent Agencies, Political Interference and Firm Investment Evidence from the European Union", http://works.bepress.com/carlo_cambini/31/.

Cambini, C. and L. Rondi (2012), "Capital structure and investment in regulated network utilities: Evidence from EU telecoms", *Industrial and Corporate Change*, Vol. 21/1, pp. 31-71.

Cubbin, J. and J. Stern (2006), "The impact of regulatory governance and privatization on electricity industry generation capacity in developing economies", *World Bank Economic Review*, Vol. 20/1, pp. 115-141.

Cukierman, A. and S. Webb (1995), "Political Influence on the Central Bank: International Evidence", *World Bank Economic Review*, Vol. 9/3, http://wber.oxfordjournals.org/content/9/3/397.short.

Dal Bo, E. (2006), "Regulatory Capture: A Review", *Oxford Review of Economic Policy*, Vol. 22/2, pp. 203-225.

Duso, T. and L.-H. Roller (2003), "Endogenous Deregulation: Evidence from OECD Countries", *Economic Letters*, Vol. 81/1, pp. 67-71.

Duso, T. and J. Seldeslachts (2010), "The political economy of mobile telecommunications liberalization: Evidence from the OECD countries", *Journal of Comparative Economics*, Vol. 38/2, pp. 199-216.

Edwards, G. and L. Waverman (2006), "The Eects of Public Ownership and Regulatory Independence on Regulatory Outcomes", *Journal of Regulatory Economics*, Vol. 29/1, pp. 23-67.

Gasmi, F. et al. (2013), "The Privatization of the Fixed-Line Telecommunications Operator in OECD, Latin America, Asia, and Africa: One Size Does Not Fit All", *World Development*, Vol. 45, pp. 189-208.

Gasmi, F., P.U. Noumba and L. Recuero Virto (2009), "Political accountability and regulatory performance in infrastructure industries: An empirical analysis", *World Bank Economic Review*, Vol. 23/3, pp. 509-531.

Gilardi, F. (2008), *Delegation in the Regulatory State: Independent Regulatory Agencies in Western Europe*, Edward Elgar Publishing, Cheltenham.

Gilardi, F. (2005a), "The Formal Independence of Regulators: A Comparison of 17 Countries and 7 Sectors", *Swiss Political Science Review*, Vol. 11/4, pp. 139-167.

Gilardi, F. (2005b), "The Institutional Foundations of Regulatory Capitalism: The Diffusion of Independent Regulatory Agencies in Western Europe", *The ANNALS of the American Academy of Political and Social Science*, Vol. 598/1, pp. 84-101.

Gilardi, F. (2002), "Policy credibility and delegation to independent regulatory agencies: a comparative empirical analysis", *Journal of European Public Policy*, Vol. 9/6, pp. 873-893.

Gilardi, F. and M. Maggetti (2010), "The independence of regulatory authorities", in *Handbook of Regulation*, Eward Elgar, Cheltenham.

Gönenç, R., M. Maher and G. Nicoletti (2000), "The Implementation and the Effects of Regulatory Reform: Past Experience and Current Issues", *OECD Economics Department Working Papers*, No. 251, OECD Publishing, Paris, http://dx.doi.org/10.1787/413754754615.

Griliches, Z. and V. Ringstad (1970), "Error-in-the-Variables Bias in Nonlinear Contexts. Econometrica", Vol. 38/2, pp. 368-370.

Gual, J. and F. Trillas (2006), "Telecommunications Policies: Measurements and Determinants", *IESE Working Paper*, No. 630, IESE Business School, University of Navarra, Barcelona, May.

Gual, J. and F. Trillas (2003), "Telecommunications Policies: Determinants and Impact", *Working Paper*, 2003/2, Institut d'Economia de Barcelona (IEB).

Guasch, J.L., J.J. Laont and S. Straub (2008), "Renegotiation of concession contracts in Latin America: Evidence from the water and transport sectors", *International Journal of Industrial Organization*, Vol. 26/2, pp. 421-442.

Gutierrez, L.H. (2003), "The Effect of Endogenous Regulation on Telecommunications Expansion and Efficiency in Latin America", *Journal of Regulatory Economics*, Vol. 23/3, pp. 257-286.

Hanretty, C., P. Larouche and A. Reindl (2012), "Independence, accountability and perceived quality of regulators: A CERRE Study", Centre on Regulaton in Europe (CERRE), Brussels, March.

Johannsen, K.S. (2003), "Regulatory Independence in Theory and Practice: A Survey of Independent Energy Regulators in Eight European Countries", AKF Forlaget, February.

Koske, I., et al. (2016), "Regulatory management practices in OECD countries", *OECD Economics Department Working Papers*, No. 1296, OECD Publishing, Paris, http://dx.doi.org/10.1787/5jm0qwm7825h-en.

Laffont, J.-J. and J. Tirole (2000), *Competition in Telecommunications*, MIT Press, Cambridge, MA.

Laffont, J.-J. and J. Tirole (1993), *A Theory of Incentives in Procurement and Regulation*, MIT Press.

Laffont, J.-J. and J. Tirole (1986), "Using cost observation to regulate firms", *Journal of Political Economy*, Vol. 94, pp. 614-641.

Levy, B. and P.T. Spiller (1994), "The Institutional Foundations of Regulatory Commitment: A Comparative Analysis of Telecommunications Regulation", *Journal of Law Economics Organization*, Vol. 10/2, pp. 201-246.

Maggetti, M. (2007), "De facto independence after delegation: A fuzzy-set analysis", *Regulation and Governance*, Vol. 1/4, pp. 271-294.

Majone, G. (1996), "Temporal Consistency and Policy Credibility: Why Democracies Need Non-Majoritarian Institutions", *EUI Working paper RSC*, Vol. 96/57, pp. 1-14.

Martin, B.L. and K. Jayakar (2013), "Moving beyond dichotomy: Comparing composite telecommunications regulatory governance indices", *Telecommunications Policy*, Vol. 37/9, pp. 691-701.

Mohammed, A.-M. and E. Strobl (2011), "Good Governance and Growth in Developing Countries: A Case Study of Regulatory Reforms in the Telecommunications Industry", *Journal of Industry, Competition and Trade*, Vol. 11/1, pp. 91-107.

Montoya, M.A. and F. Trillas (2007), "The measurement of the independence of telecommunications regulatory agencies in Latin America and the Caribbean", *Utilities Policy*, Vol. 15/3, pp. 182-190.

Murillo, M.V. and A. Post (2014), "Revisiting the Obsolescing Bargain in Post-Crisis Argentina: Investor Portfolios and Regulatory Outcomes", UC Berkeley and Columbia University.

OECD (2015a), *OECD Regulatory Policy Outlook 2015*, OECD Publishing, Paris, http://dx.doi.org/10.1787/9789264238770-en.

OECD (2015b), *The Governance of Water Regulators*, OECD Studies on Water, OECD Publishing, Paris, http://dx.doi.org/10.1787/9789264231092-en.

OECD (2014), *The Governance of Regulators*, OECD Best Practice Principles for Regulatory Policy, OECD Publishing, Paris, http://dx.doi.org/10.1787/9789264209015-en.

OECD (n.d.), "PMR Indicators of Product Market Regulation", www.oecd.org/economy/growth/indicatorsofproductmarketregulationhomepage.htm.

Ros, A.J. (1999), "Does Ownership or Competition Matter? The Effects of Telecommunications Reform on Network Expansion and Eciency", *Journal of Regulatory Economics*, Vol. 15/1, p. 92.

Stern, J. (1997), "What Makes an Independent Regulator Independent?", *Business Strategy Review* Vol. 8/2, pp. 67-74.

Spiegel, Y. and D.F. Spulber (1994), *The RAND Journal of Economics*, Vol. 25/3, Autumn, pp. 424-440, www.jstor.org/stable/2555770?seq=1#page_scan_tab_contents.

Stigler, G.J. (1971), The Theory of Economic Regulation", *The Bell Journal of Economics and Management Science*, Vol. 2/1, pp. 3-21.

Sutherland, D. et al. (2011), "Public Policies and Investment in Network Infrastructure", *OECD Journal: Economic Studies*, Vol. 2011/1, http://dx.doi.org/10.1787/eco_studies-2011-5kg51mlvk6r6.

Trillas, F. (2010), "Independent Regulators: Theory, Evidence and Reform Proposals", *IESE Business School Working Paper*, WP-860, May.

Trillas, F. and M.A. Montoya (2013), "Independent regulators: theory, evidence and reform proposals", *Info*, Vol. 15/3, pp.39-53.

Trillas, F. and M.A. Montoya (2009), "Commitment and Regulatory Independence in Practice in Latin American and Caribbean Countries", *Competition and Regulation in Network Industries*, Intersentia, Vol. 12/1, pp. 27-57, March.

Trillas, F. and M.A. Montoya (2008), "The Degree of Commitment to Regulator Independence: Measurement and Impact", *Working Paper Series Centro Asia Pacific*, www.ief.es/documentos/recursos/publicaciones/revistas/hac_pub/185_Degree.pdf.

Ugur, M. (2009), "Regulatory Quality and Performance in EU Network Industries: Evidence on Telecommunications, Gas and Electricity", *Journal of Public Policy*, Vol. 29/3, pp. 347-370.

Viscusi, W., J. Harrington Jr. and J.M. Vernon (2005), "Introduction to Economic Regulation", in *Economics of Regulation and Antitrust, Fourth edition*, pp. 357-399, MIT Press, Cambridge.

Waverman, L. and P. Koutroumpis (2011), "Benchmarking telecoms regulation the Telecommunications Regulatory Governance Index (TRGI)", *Telecommunications Policy*, Vol. 35/5, pp. 450-468.

Zhelyazkova, N. (2016a), "The Independence of Regulatory Agencies in Network Industries: Literature Review", *Working Paper of the Chair of Governance and Regulation,* Dauphine University, Paris, forthcoming.

Zhelyazkova, N. (2016b), "How do regulatory networks contribute to regulatory independence?", *Working Paper of the Chair of Governance and Regulation,* Dauphine University, Paris, forthcoming.

Zhelyazkova, N. (2016c), "Regulatory Independence in the European Union", *Working Paper of the Chair of Governance and Regulation,* Dauphine University, Paris, forthcoming.

ORGANISATION FOR ECONOMIC CO-OPERATION AND DEVELOPMENT

The OECD is a unique forum where governments work together to address the economic, social and environmental challenges of globalisation. The OECD is also at the forefront of efforts to understand and to help governments respond to new developments and concerns, such as corporate governance, the information economy and the challenges of an ageing population. The Organisation provides a setting where governments can compare policy experiences, seek answers to common problems, identify good practice and work to co-ordinate domestic and international policies.

The OECD member countries are: Australia, Austria, Belgium, Canada, Chile, the Czech Republic, Denmark, Estonia, Finland, France, Germany, Greece, Hungary, Iceland, Ireland, Israel, Italy, Japan, Korea, Luxembourg, Mexico, the Netherlands, New Zealand, Norway, Poland, Portugal, the Slovak Republic, Slovenia, Spain, Sweden, Switzerland, Turkey, the United Kingdom and the United States. The European Union takes part in the work of the OECD.

OECD Publishing disseminates widely the results of the Organisation's statistics gathering and research on economic, social and environmental issues, as well as the conventions, guidelines and standards agreed by its members.